TILES

Souvenir Press Collectors Guide Series
Mugs and Tankards, by Deborah Stratton
Jugs by James Paton
Buttons by Victor Houart
Easter Eggs by Victor Houart
Lamps by James Paton

TILES

—A Collector's Guide

by Hans van Lemmen

SOUVENIR PRESS

First published 1979 by Souvenir Press Ltd,
43 Great Russell Street, London WC1B 3PA
and simultaneously in Canada

Book designed by PAMELA MARA

ISBN 0 285 62408 3

Filmset and printed in Great Britain by
BAS Printers Limited, Over Wallop, Hampshire

CONTENTS

For Patsy, Johanna and Miranda.

ACKNOWLEDGEMENTS

I wish to thank the following people and institutions who have directly or indirectly made it possible for me to write this book.

Mr. A. Garlick, Assistant Keeper, Abbey House Museum, Leeds; Mr. G. Deslandes, Keeper of Art, Dundee Museums and Art Galleries; Mr. N. Law, Regional Councillor, Tayside Region; Mr. J. Rumsby, Keeper of Archaeology, Hull Museums and Art Galleries; Dr. C. Hammond, Secretary of the Victorian Society, West Yorkshire Group; and Mr. D. Richards, Lecturer in Ceramics, Leeds Polytechnic.

The Gladstone Pottery Museum, Longton, Stoke-on-Trent; the Minton Museum, Stoke-on-Trent; the Ironbridge Gorge Museum, Telford; the Bradford Industrial Museum; the Manchester City Art Gallery; the Abbey House Museum, Leeds; the Cincinnati Art Museum, Ohio; the Tile Museum 'It Noflik Sté', Otterlo, Holland; the John Taylor Teachers' Centre, Leeds; Leeds Central Library; and the Central Library in Stoke-on-Trent.

My special thanks are due to Mr. G. K. Beaulah who made many of his tiles available for reproduction and who has made many valuable comments throughout the writing of this book.

INTRODUCTION

Amongst all the Victoriana that has become so desirable as collectors' items in recent years—the jugs, teapots, plates and ornaments of all kinds—the qualities of the decorated ceramic tiles of the Victorian and Edwardian period have increasingly become recognised and sought after. For while tiles are attractive and fascinating to collect, they have the great advantage that, far from being an expensive rarity, they are numerous enough to have remained relatively cheap.

Nineteenth-century potteries, enjoying the benefits of new mass-production techniques, were able to cater for a demand for tiles that led to their being used in all kinds of places—from town halls to signposts; from fire-places to furniture. And the designers responded with such a variety of themes and colours that there is something of interest to every modern collector. Styles from the past such as the Renaissance and the Gothic are found next to designs inspired by the Arts and Crafts movement, Art Nouveau, even the Far East.

Finding out about the date of the tiles you buy, their manufacturers and the way in which they were made and decorated will add to the pleasure of having a tile collection and will also be profitable, since a knowledgeable collector can be selective in what he buys, when he goes hunting through antique shops and markets.

An understanding of the history of tile-making in Britain, from the Middle Ages to Delftware, will help the collector appreciate the development that took place in the last century. This guide has been written on the basis of practical experience, and I hope that the information, suggestions and tips will be of value both to the new and to the more experienced tile collector.

COLLECTING TILES

Still freely available and relatively cheap, tiles from the Victorian and Edwardian period offer the richest field of interest to the collector. This is due to the enormous expansion in the British tile industry during the second half of the nineteenth century, when mechanisation allowed tiles to be produced in greater quantity and with more variety in technique and design than ever before.

There were earlier times during which tiles were used a great deal in Britain—particularly the Middle Ages. You can still see such early tiles on the floors of many churches and cathedrals, as well as in museums, but they do not come on to the open market. Later on, Dutch and English Delftware tiles became popular in pre-mass production days, but examples of these have become very expensive now.

The Victorians liked the decorative and hard-wearing qualities of tiles, and they were used in buildings on a large scale—in kitchens and bathrooms, on fireplaces, floors and sometimes on the outside of the house, too.

Certain shops, such as butchers and fishmongers, were tiled throughout for hygiene, while entrance halls and public rooms of municipal buildings were tiled for easy maintenance and for the added touch of splendour.

When these Victorian, and the later Edwardian, buildings are demolished, the tiles that remain intact find their way into antique shops, markets and salerooms. Many more tiles have been destroyed than saved during demolition work, although lately the contractors have become more aware of their value. At times it is possible to get hold of some from these sites, with permission from the contractor.

The really determined collector can pick up quite a number of tiles in this way, and he has the added advantage of being able to date the tiles by the age of the building, as well as knowing the way in which they were being used—for fire surround, or kitchen, or whatever. Of course, this requires being in the right place at the right time.

Tiles were also often set into furniture, such as washstands. If the piece is in poor condition, the tiles can easily be removed.

Collectors hunting through antique shops, markets and salerooms will find that prices will depend on many factors. A dealer may ask more for tiles that have such names as Minton or Wedgwood on the back—they are not necessarily better than those by other manufacturers, but the names command respect in the antique trade. However, it is worth trying to bargain if you think the price is too high.

You will have to pay more for a complete set with special subject-matter, such as the Minton tiles with Shakespearean scenes, historical romantic themes and finely printed or painted animals and portraits. Much less expensive, but very colourful and attractive, are the ordinary tiles with floral patterns.

Markets are good hunting-grounds for tiles because often more than one stall will be offering them for sale, so that you can compare prices and find the best bargains. The prices here are very often lower than elsewhere.

Some dealers will look out for tiles for regular customers, and may even be prepared to find special types of tiles, so it is worth letting them know of your interest.

Salerooms are a different matter as auctioneers do not sell single tiles except as part of a mixed lot. Sometimes, however, there may be a whole box for sale and if you find that there are a few of similar design, these spares or doubles can be used to exchange for others in antique shops. It is worth swopping two tiles bought in a sale for one good example in an antique shop if the dealer is willing to enter into that kind of arrangement.

There are many ways in which you can build up your collection, and if you are determined, discerning—and at times, lucky—it is amazing how quickly it will grow.

An antique shop window with a selection of tiles for sale.

MEDIEVAL TILES

Although the history of tile-making goes back to Egyptian, Babylonian and Assyrian times, decorative tiles were first introduced into the British Isles during the Middle Ages when they were used to pave the floors of abbey churches, cathedral chapter houses and royal palaces.

The word 'tile' is derived from the Latin *tegula* and is formed from the verb *tegere* which means 'to cover'. The Romans used the word *tegula* to indicate a piece of fired clay that was used in covering buildings, and the English 'tile' applies similarly to all forms of plain or decorated, glazed or unglazed slabs of baked clay used to cover buildings for functional or decorative purposes.

The Babylonians and Assyrians in particular developed the craft of tile-making for artistic purposes, using glazes whose colours included blues, yellows, reds and greens as well as black and white. With them they created picture panels and geometric designs for the walls of their ornate palaces and temples.

Unglazed tiles were used in large numbers by the Greeks and Romans to cover floors, roofs and friezes, but after the fall of the Roman Empire there was a lull in tile-making until the Muslims began to use them for their mosques. It was their tradition of decorated tiles that reached Northern Europe, partly through the Crusades and trade routes, but mainly via Italy from Moorish-occupied Spain.

The thirteenth century saw the first flowering in Britain of a period of tile production that lasted until the beginning of the sixteenth century. At that time the dissolution of the monasteries, together with a change in the fashion of floor decoration, ensured the virtual end of the medieval era of the tile industry.

Despite the ravages of time, there are many excellent examples of

Mosaic tile made in 9 sections forming the shape of a four petalled flower, Meaux Abbey, c. 1250. *Collection G. K. Beaulah.*

medieval tiles that have survived and can still be seen *in situ* as well as in museums. You will find that, because of inconsistencies in mixing clay, the varying quality of the lead glazes and uncertainty in the firing, no tile is exactly like another, and this adds to their charm.

Medieval tiles are usually $4\frac{1}{2}$ inches (11·5 cm) across and can be up to 1 inch (2·5 cm) thick. They are limited in colour because they depend for their variety simply on differently coloured clays and relatively few tinted glazes. The clays are red and white and were often used in the form of a red tile with an inlaid decoration of white clay. Another variation was achieved by covering the tile with a clear lead glaze, for after firing the red clay turned brown and the white clay, yellow, to give the characteristic medieval brown tile with yellow decoration.

Lead glaze was the one used for medieval tiles, and by adding oxides it was possible to obtain a few different colours. A lead glaze to which a little copper has been added will look light green on white

Mosaic tile made in 6 sections showing a pair of stylised doves, Meaux Abbey, c. 1250. *Collection: G. K. Beaulah.*

clay and dark green over red clay, while a high proportion of copper resulted in black. In England it was customary to apply glaze to the tile before firing.

Although medieval tiles are somewhat restricted in their colour, their decoration can be very rich in form, with rampant lions, dragons, knights on horseback, birds, heraldic and human figures as well as abstract patterns.

This great variety of patterns and themes is best studied by visiting sites that have medieval tiles *in situ*, such as Byland Abbey in Yorkshire, Cleeve Abbey in Somerset or Melrose Abbey in

Roxburghshire. One of the most complete surviving floors is found in the Chapter House of Westminster Abbey. The Abbey was built under the patronage of Henry III and the floor of the Chapter House, which was built between 1246 and 1253, would have been put in towards the end of the building operations. The tiles were made at the Benedictine Abbey of Chertsey, and the so-called Chertsey Tiles rank among the best medieval tiles produced. They have inlaid patterns and figures, the best known among them being those showing Henry III seated on a throne and his wife, Queen Eleanor, with a falcon on her wrist; others display the royal arms and hunting scenes, and there is also a nice border tile that shows a pike or salmon.

When medieval tiles are looked at from a technical standpoint, it is possible to distinguish four basic methods of decoration: mosaic, inlaid and printed decorations, and relief patterning.

The mosaics were made from small pieces of fired clay that were assembled into a great variety of patterns based on geometry and symmetry. It was also possible to make more complex designs, either with simple bird shapes cut in one piece, or of fleur-de-lis made out of several sections.

Different colours could be created by covering the top of each piece with slip (thin liquid clay) and lead glaze.

Many mosaic floors have a distinctly eastern flavour, which is not surprising when one remembers that at the time when the first mosaic floors were being laid in Britain, there was already a well-established

Left: Inlaid tile with a rampant lion in a circle, 13th century. *Collection: G. K. Beaulah.*

Right: Inlaid tile with fleur-de-lis, Nottingham kiln, 14th century. *Collection: G. K. Beaulah.*

tradition of decorative tiles in the Middle East whose influence had spread to Europe.

The technique of producing inlaid tiles was introduced into England at the beginning of the thirteenth century, probably from France. Inlaid tiles were made by stamping a pattern into the clay and filling the resulting depression with slip. Usually the tile was made from red firing clay, and the inlaid decoration was white. It was dried and covered with lead glaze before being fired so that after firing the result was a brown tile with inlaid yellow decoration.

After so long, the glaze on many medieval tiles has been worn away, but deeply inlaid tiles still show their decoration, even after extensive wear.

The printed tiles are actually an odd combination of printing and inlay. There is still some uncertainty about the printing process, but

Tile showing a hound eating from a plate, made at York, late 15th century. *Collection: G. K. Beaulah.*

Tile with an impressed pattern, Meaux Abbey, 15th century. *Collection: G. K. Beaulah.*

it was probably done with a piece of wood with raised pattern that was dipped in slip and then pressed on to the surface of the tile. The layer of slip would be thin and prone to wear, but during the fourteenth century many tiles were produced in this way as it was a method that saved time and so was suited to production on a moderately large scale.

There are some printed tiles that have their decoration pressed slightly below the surface, and so are better protected against wear. This type could also have been made by brushing the whole tile with slip, imprinting the pattern and then scraping the slip from the top.

Relief tiles have sunken relief, or a more elaborate raised pattern, and they were covered with transparent lead glaze. They relied on the clay itself for their colour, and on light to set off the relief pattern.

The collector of Victorian tiles will find that the study of medieval examples, especially the inlaid types, will repay him, as this was a style that was revived, along with other Gothic characteristics, in the nineteenth century.

DUTCH AND ENGLISH DELFTWARE TILES

In Holland, too, it was customary during the Middle Ages to use decorative floor tiles, particularly in ecclesiastical building; but at the beginning of the sixteenth century the medieval floor tile was superseded by the painted majolica tile from Italy.

By the sixteenth century the Italians already had a well established tradition of decorating pavements and walls with painted tiles, and when the Renaissance began to spread north during the first half of the century, the tradition of painted tiles went with it.

An Italian potter, Guido da Savino, set up a pottery in Antwerp at this time, and one of his sons later established his own pottery in Middelburg, Zealand.

While the medieval floor tiles depended for their decoration on differently coloured clay and lead glaze, majolica tiles derived their colour from the application of high-temperature ceramic colours on to tin glaze: the word *majolica* comes from 'Majorca', the Mediterranean island, which was an important centre for tin-glazed earthenware during the fifteenth century. The colours on majolica ware range from orange, blue and yellow to brown and purple.

Dutch potters soon began to produce similar ware, and we can still see early Flemish and Dutch tiles with abstract patterns in orange, dark blue, green and yellow on a white ground that are reminiscent of Moorish designs.

Four tiles were usually needed to form one pattern, and the bold quality of their design made them very suitable for wall decoration. A particular feature of these early tiles is the 'reserving' technique, whereby the outline of a pattern was drawn on to the tile, and the background painted in, leaving the pattern white on a dark ground.

At the end of the sixteenth century the Dutch craftsmen began to

Panel of 16 Dutch tiles, four tiles are needed to form one pattern, blue, amber and green, early 17th century. *Tile museum 'It Noflik Sté' Otterlo, Holland.*

introduce new motifs, such as portraits, bowls of fruit, soldiers and animal figures, and these were still painted in a variety of colours.

During the first half of the seventeenth century, the Dutch tile industry became firmly established throughout Holland. It began in Rotterdam as early as 1590, soon spreading to Haarlem, Delft, Gouda, Utrecht and later to Friesland, where Harlingen and Makkum became important centres. The Makkum factory is still active today, and has been kept in the same family since the middle of the seventeenth century.

Holland's trade links with the far East meant that Chinese porcelain too influenced Dutch potters. The fashion of the time for blue and white porcelain was reflected in the Dutch tile, where a blue decoration on a white ground began to replace multi-coloured patterns, and the tile painter would sometimes copy Chinese motifs.

Left: Dutch tile based on a Moorish pattern, blue, amber and red-brown, late 16th century. *Tile museum 'It Noflik Sté', Otterlo, Holland.*

Right: Dutch tile showing a flower, blue, amber and green, fleur-de-lis corner ornaments, first half 17th century. *Collection: G. K. Beaulah.*

The second half of the seventeenth century also saw the influence of Dutch painting and engraving on the decoration of tiles. Many painters had turned to their environment as a source of subjects, and the tile designer took up similar themes. In blue or manganese, the tiles were now painted with horsemen, ships, landscapes, flowers, birds, children at play and shepherds with their sheep, as well as scenes from the Old and New Testaments.

These themes continued well into the eighteenth century and their great popularity meant that they were exported all over Europe.

In Holland itself, tiles were used for fireplaces, kitchens, cellars, window-sills and wall skirting, and in certain cases whole rooms were tiled from top to bottom. In the background of Vermeer's *The Kitchen Maid* you will see tiles forming the wall skirting, and there are more examples in other seventeenth-century Dutch paintings.

Important commissions for Dutch craftsmen came from abroad. These included the tiled room, with individual tiles and complete panels, in the Château de Rambouillet near Paris, and the kitchen for the Amalienburg Pavillion at Schloss Nymphenburg near Munich.

Collectors should note that each tile usually has its picture framed within a quadrate, circle, octagon or other decorative border, and a small ornamental motif at each corner. These motifs may be in the form of fleur-de-lis, ox heads, spider's heads, Wan-lis, carnations and many other variations.

Another characteristic of the Dutch tile is the pinhole indentation at each corner. These were made when it was cut to size, using a square board and a knife. In each corner of the board were one or more little nails which prevented the board from slipping during the cutting process.

After the tiles had been cut they were spread out under cover, and when sufficiently dry they were fired. A first firing is known as a biscuit firing, and the fired tile blanks themselves are called 'biscuits'.

Before the tiles were glazed they were brushed clean and immersed in water, which prevented too much moisture from the glaze being absorbed by the tile. Tin glaze was used—that is, lead glaze to which tin has been added, the tin producing a white and opaque effect.

When the glaze was dry the tile could be painted. The drawing was put on to the tile by 'pouncing'—that is, a piece of paper with the design pricked out was put over the tile, and charcoal brushed

Dutch tile with a soldier in 16th century dress, blue, first half 17th century. *Collection: G. K. Beaulah.*

Some typical corner ornaments which appear on Dutch tiles. Each type of ornament can be found in many 17th and 18th century variations.

MOORISH MOTIF

FLEUR-DE-LIS

WAN-LI

CARNATION

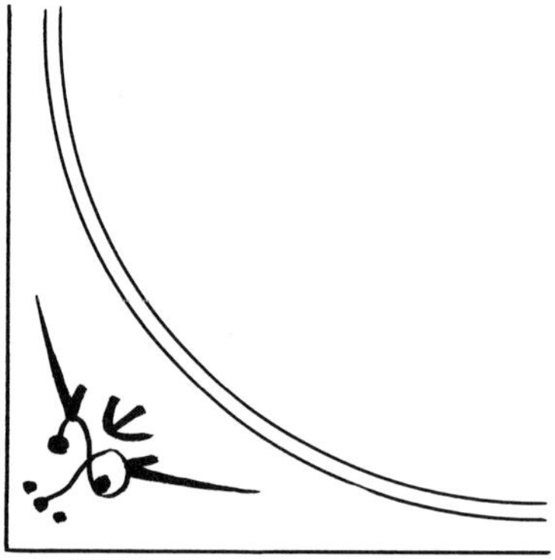
OX-HEAD

SPIDER'S HEAD

over the paper and through the holes. The painter then traced the outlines of the drawing on to the tile with paint, and added the finishing colours or tones. After this the tile was fired again.

Sometimes a third firing was necessary if colours were added that could not stand high temperatures. These were put on after the second firing as enamels, and fired at a low temperature (*petit-feu*) in a muffle-kiln.

The Dutch tile industry remained relatively prosperous until the middle of the eighteenth century. But by then English Delftware was competing for the market, and the second half of the century saw a gradual decline in the output and sometimes the quality of the Dutch tile.

The manufacturers encountered foreign competition together with a change in the fashion of interior decoration, in which wallpaper posed the major threat. The Napoleonic wars meant an even more restricted market and by the middle of the nineteenth century most potteries had closed down or stopped making tiles, although the tradition of making them never died out completely.

In England, the flowering of Delftware during the eighteenth century lasted only until the invention of transfer printing in the 1750s. The name 'English Delftware' is itself an indication of the strong link with Dutch tiles. The term however is not a very satisfactory one because the majority of Dutch tiles had in fact been produced in centres outside Delft. But since the name 'Delft' had already become well known for pottery other than tiles—plates,

Below left: Dutch tile showing a sailing boat, blue, ox-head corner ornaments, first half 17th century. *Collection: G. K. Beaulah.*

Below right: Dutch tile showing Cain slaying Abel, blue, ox-head corner ornaments, first half 18th century. *Collection: G. K. Beaulah.*

Left: Dutch tile with a landscape, manganese, ox-head corner ornaments, late 18th century. *Collection: Author.*

Right: Dutch tile showing a man on horseback, manganese, late 18th century. *Collection: Author.*

dishes, vases and jugs, both multi-coloured and in the familiar 'blue-and-white' famous throughout Europe—and Delft tiles, in particular the landscape designs, were of very high quality, it is perhaps understandable that in England those imported from Holland became associated with the name.

Dutch potters introduced tin-glazed earthenware into England during the second half of the sixteenth century, but it was not until the last two decades of the century that serious attempts were made to produce English Delftware in London. There is some documentary evidence concerning a Dutch potter called Van Hamme who was granted a patent in 1676 for the 'Art of Makeinge Tiles and Porcelane and other Earthen Wares, after the way practiced in Holland'.

Technical difficulties meant that it was not possible to make enough English Delftware to meet demand, so Dutch tiles continued to be imported despite a ban imposed in 1672 on the import of foreign pottery. In the first half of the eighteenth century we find several potteries in Lambeth making Delftware based on Dutch designs in commercial quantity.

Bristol is another centre where tiles were produced and it would seem that a fair number of those with Biblical subjects came from there. Liverpool was the third important centre, though it began making them later than London or Bristol. Dutch tiles were imported into Britain through Liverpool, but despite this influence Liverpool designs and colours are much more varied than their Dutch counterparts.

It is not easy to make a distinction between examples of London, Bristol and Liverpool ware, although identification has become somewhat easier after excavations carried out on pottery sites in those towns, for broken tile fragments can provide valuable information about their manufacture and composition.

More noticeable differences occur between Dutch and English tiles: Dutch examples have a tin glaze that is whiter than that on most English tiles, which have a bluish tinge. English tiles on the other hand

Panel of 6 Dutch tiles showing a parrot, polychrome, second half 18th century. *Tile museum 'It Noflik Sté', Otterlo, Holland.*

can have a richer, glossier glaze caused by a higher lead content. A particular English feature is the *bianco-sopra-bianco* border ornament found on certain tiles. The term means 'white on white' and is a border in pure white on the slightly-tinted white body glaze, which can be a very pleasing decorative addition. There are some very fine Bristol examples with this feature.

The production of English Delftware underwent a transformation when John Sadler with the aid of Guy Green in Liverpool invented the technique of transfer printing.

In an affidavit of July 27th 1756, John Sadler and Guy Green take oath that they 'without the aid or assistance of any other person or persons, did within the space of six hours, to wit, between the hours of nine in the morning and three in the afternoon of the same day, print upwards of twelve hundred Earthenware tiles of different patterns, at Liverpoole aforesaid, and which, as these deponents have heard and believe, were more in number and better and neater than one hundred skilful pot-painters could have painted in the like space of time, in the common and usual way painting with pencil; and these deponents say that they have been upwards of seven years in finding out the method of printing tiles, and in making tryals and

Left: English Delftware tile from Lambeth showing a coastal scene, blue and manganese, cornflower corner ornaments, mid 18th century. *Collection: G. K. Beaulah.*

Right: Delftware tile from Bristol showing a coastal scene, blue and manganese, oriental style corner ornaments, first half 18th century. *Collection: G. K. Beaulah.*

English Delftware tile from Bristol with a river scene, exceptionally fine painting, blue, mid 18th century.
Collection: G. K. Beaulah.

English Delftware tile from Liverpool with a stylised anemone, blue, second half 18th century.
Collection: G. K. Beaulah.

Sadler and Green tile showing Mr. Moody as Simon in *Harlequin's Invasion*. John Moody was a comedian excelling in Irish characters. The tile has a border of theatrical trophies and was probably made during the 1760s. *Manchester City Art Gallery (ref. no. 1923.354).*

experiments for that purpose, which they have now through great paine and expense brought to perfection.'

It is not certain who invented the actual technique first, but one does know that in 1756 Sadler and Green had perfected the technique of transfer printing to such an extent that they were ready to go into business. During the first year they took prints from woodblocks, but in 1757 they began to use copper plates.

The process consisted of printing on to the fired glaze of a tile by means of a transfer tissue. A print was taken from a woodblock or copper plate on a thin piece of paper, using an ink consisting of ceramic colour mixed with oil which would help the ink to stick to the surface of the tile. The paper was put on to the surface of the tile,

Sadler and Green tile showing Mrs. Ward in the character of Rodogune. Mrs. Ward first appeared on stage in Liverpool and later acted at Covent Garden, London. The tile has a border of theatrical trophies and was probably made during the 1760s. *Manchester City Art Gallery (ref. no. 1923.354).*

ink side down, and rubbed down firmly before being soaked off again, leaving the ink behind. The tile was then fired at a low temperature which fixed the printed design on firmly.

Sadler tiles range widely in subject matter, the most numerous being open-air scenes in which figures of the *haute monde*, of decided French flavour, posture elegantly in the costume of shepherdess or dandy. Other themes to be found are Aesop's fables, ships, games, landscapes with romantic ruins and, perhaps most interesting of all, portraits of actors and actresses of the English theatre. These are often portrayed in a particular rôle on the stage, and bear the name of the actor and the title of the play, which makes them of considerable historical interest.

Sadler and Green tile with a representation of one of Aesop's fables, the Wolf and the Sow. The tile has a border of rococo scrolls and was probably made during the 1760s. *Manchester City Art Gallery (ref. no. 1923.352/53).*

Sadler and Green tile showing the game of Blind's Man Buff. The tile has an elaborate border of rococo scrolls and other motifs, c. 1760. *Collection: G. K. Beaulah.*

Sadler's tiles were printed in a variety of colours, including blue, dark red and black, and some have his name on the front.

The invention of transfer printing had considerable consequences for the tile industry as a whole. Printed tiles soon became powerful rivals to those painted by hand, for hand painting was a time-consuming business, and therefore expensive. Printing was quick and efficient, and the decoration could be fixed with a low-temperature firing which made their production even cheaper. Transfer printing was also a necessary precursor to the mechanisation of tile production in the second half of the nineteenth century.

The differences between a printed tile and a painted tile can clearly be seen. *Above:* a detail from a Sadler and Green tile with its delicately engraved lines and *below:* a detail of a hand-painted Dutch tile showing the fluency and directness of the brush.

VICTORIAN TILE PRODUCTION AND DECORATION TECHNIQUES

Victorian tiles were made of either plastic or dust-pressed clay. The first is ordinary clay to which enough water has been added to make it plastic, or malleable. It was rolled out in slabs and cut into squares and then allowed to dry slowly before being fired.

Dust-pressed tiles were made from powdered clay which had a low moisture content and was pressed into shape by machine. This technique was invented by Richard Prosser, who patented the idea in 1840. The manufacturer Herbert Minton, realising its potential, bought a share of the patent; for dust-pressing is quick and efficient, and does not need the long drying period of plastic clay. It also shrinks less readily and so is less likely to warp during firing.

The dust-pressed tile is easy to recognise, as it is smooth and white and usually has a pattern of bars or squares pressed into the back—this was to hold the cement or plaster used when the tile was stuck on to a wall. Most tiles made after 1840 were of this type. At first the machines used were hand-operated, but in 1873 Maw and Co. introduced the first steam-driven press.

Most Victorian tiles are six inches square, border tiles measuring six by three inches. Occasionally tiles were made eight inches square, or six by twelve inches. The widest variety of size and shape is found in floor tiles, which can be round or triangular as well as rectangular.

The expansion of the tile industry also meant the development of new methods of decorating tiles, and these were used increasingly alongside the more traditional ways. The Victorians used hand painting, slip painting, tube lining, sgraffito, transfer printing, moulding, inlay and aerography.

Plastic clay tiles usually had a white glaze put on to make an even surface to paint on, but this was not necessary with the dust-pressed

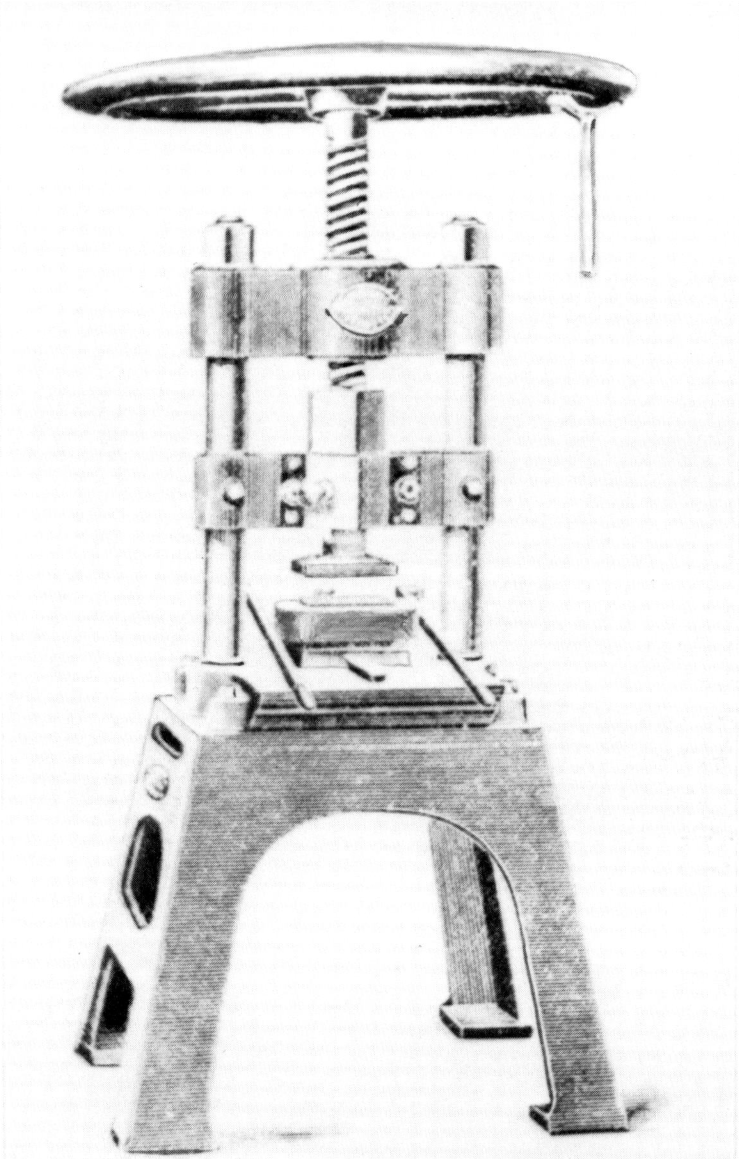

The clay dust press transformed the tile industry. A press like this could produce over 1000 tiles per day.

ones, which already had a smooth white clay surface that would take painting or printing. Handpainting was done either in a single colour or in several, and it always has a boldness that contrasts sharply with printed or moulded designs.

Sgraffito tiles, which are very rare, were made with two layers of contrasting slip. The top layer was scratched away to reveal the colour of the underlying slip, forming the figure and contrasting ground. This technique can be compared with that of scraper board. Some excellent examples were made by the well known designer and pottery-decorator M. L. Solon, who worked for Minton.

Slip decoration falls into two categories: first, there is the method in which coloured slip in a bag was pressed through a metal nozzle, very much like icing on a cake. After the decoration had been applied to the unfired tile it was fired, a clear glaze applied, and then fired again.

The other method is also known as 'tube lining'. Thin lines were piped on to the tiles following a previously outlined drawing, and after firing the areas between the raised lines of slip were filled with translucent glazes and the tile was fired a second time. The translucent glazes were also referred to as majolica glazes, and so the tile was known as a majolica tile. Like hand painting and sgraffito, slip decoration was done entirely by hand.

John Sadler's transfer printing technique was used increasingly in the nineteenth century to decorate mass produced tiles. The Victorians took their transfers from an engraved copper or zinc plate, or from a design done on a lithographic stone. In both cases the

A transfer tissue with two prints ready for transfer on to a biscuit fired tile. *The Gladstone Pottery Museum, Stoke-on-Trent.*

Hand-painted tile with acorns, oak leaves and quarter star and sun in opposite corners, green, yellow, blue and black, c. 1875, no marks. *Collection: Author.*

printing involves the transfer of the design from metal plate or stone on to the tiles by means of a transfer tissue a thin piece of paper on which the design was printed in colour mixed with oil which was removed from the tile after the design had been applied. After the firing, which removed the oil, the design could be coloured in by hand before the tile was covered with a transparent glaze and the last firing given.

Unlike Sadler's transfer prints, which were put on top of the glaze, the Victorian ones were usually put directly onto the biscuit fired tile and then glazed—a process known as under-glaze decoration. Prints taken from copper and zinc plates were most suitable for fine line work, while those from lithographic stones were best for larger areas of colour.

Moulded tiles were produced by using a metal or plaster die in the dust-pressing process. After the biscuit firing the tile, with its design in relief, was painted with translucent or opaque majolica glazes and fired again—stacked horizontally to prevent the glazes from running.

Some moulded tiles had a single glaze, others more than one; and they could also be produced in varying degrees of relief. It was also possible mechanically to produce thin raised lines which are reminiscent of the tube-lining process. Moulded tiles often have a rich surface texture when the uneven surface covered with translucent or opaque glazes catches and reflects the light.

One of the specialities of Minton and Maw and Co. was the making of inlaid or encaustic tiles, that had a pattern of differently coloured clays inlaid and fired at a high temperature. Herbert Minton revived this medieval idea with the encouragement of the Gothic Revival architect A. W. N. Pugin. At first Minton experimented with inlaid

Sgraffito tile with an allegorical representation of the pottery industry, buff and black, made by M. L. Solon for Minton, c. 1887. *The City Museum and Art Gallery, Stoke-on-Trent.*

Tube-lined tile with an Art Nouveau design decorated with translucent glazes in shades of green, c. 1905, made by H. & R. Johnson. *Collection: G. K. Beaulah.*

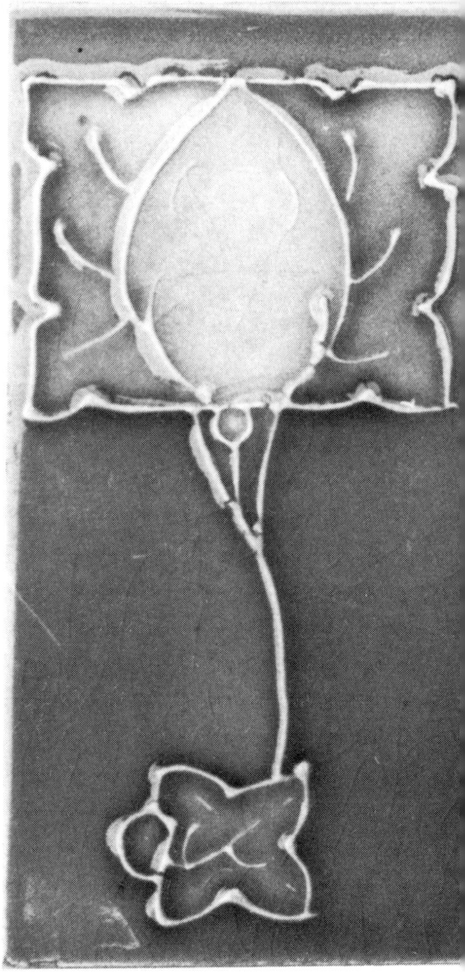

tiles made from plastic clay pressed into a plaster mould, so that when the tile was removed the design was left in the clay. This impressed pattern was then filled with clay of a different colour, dried and fired at a high temperature.

In 1863 William Boulton and Joseph Worthington took out a patent for the manufacture of dust-pressed encaustic tiles which were made in a reverse process: a brass plate was made with a cut-out inlay pattern, and the clay was pressed through the plate and into the base of the mould; so that when the plate was removed the inlaid design was left lying face down in the bottom of the metal mould. The mould was then filled with powdered clay which was pressed down to form the main body of the tile.

Above left: Slip-painted tile with a pattern based on strawberries and leaves, brown-red, green and black, covered with an ochre tinged translucent glaze, c. 1880, raised letter H on the back. *Collection: Author.*
Above right: Transfer printed tile with a print taken from a copper-plate engraving showing two blue tits in a landscape with reeds and water, black print on a buff ground, signed in bottom left corner L. T. Swetnam, c. 1890, on the back in raised letters MINTONS CHINA WORKS STOKE ON TRENT. *Collection: Author.*

Below left: Transfer printed tile with a print taken from a lithographic stone, chrysanthemum and leaves in white on a dark blue ground, c. 1892, on the back in raised letters CRAVEN DUNNILL & CO JACKFIELD SALOP. *Collection: Author.*
Below right: Moulded tile with a simple stylised flower within a square border, blue, raised letter P on the back, made by Pilkington. *Collection: Author.*

Moulded tile with a design in relief of two arum lilies in white, green, red, yellow, brown and ochre-grey translucent glazes, on the back is the printed registration number Rd. 67048, registered in 1887 by the Decorative Art Tile Co. Ltd, Hanley. *Collection: Author.*

Unglazed mosaic floor tile with a small dust-pressed inlaid tile in the centre, mosaic tiles in dark brown and green, inlaid tile has a black cross on a white ground, c. 1880, no marks. *Collection: Author*

Left: Glazed inlaid tile for church use, buff coloured fleur-de-lis inlaid in black, c. 1880, on the back in incised letters THE CAMPBELL BRICK & TILE CO. STOKE ON TRENT. *Collection: Author.*

Right: Unglazed tile with an impressed pseudo-mosaic pattern based on a fleur-de-lis in red-brown, ochre and white, on the back in raised letters CRAVEN DUNNILL, c. 1885. *Collection: Author.*

Tile manufacturers did some ingenious things with dust-pressed encaustic tiles. One invention was the making of pseudo mosaic. The various coloured clays, which were pressed first, were pushed on to a plate with ridges resembling a mosaic pattern, so that when the tile was finished and removed from the press it had deeply incised lines over the whole surface in mosaic fashion.

The tiles were used as floor tiles, and when the grooves were filled with cement or grouting the resemblance to mosaic was complete. One wonders how many Victorian 'mosaic' floors were made in this way. The two firms producing these tiles were Maw and Co. and Craven Dunnill.

Aerography was also used only for decorating tiles. A stencil was placed over the tile and ceramic colour blown on with an aerograph or air-brush. The aerograph was a metal tube with a nozzle and container for the colour. Air was forced through with a foot-pump, or mechanically, and both fine lines or broad areas of colour could be sprayed on, depending on the size of the nozzle.

Tile with a brown decoration of a stylised grapevine executed with stencil and aerograph, c. 1890, no marks. *Collection: Author.*

Colour applied with an aerograph can be detected only by close scrutiny, when it can be seen that the sprayed areas show fine stipples or specks.

At times one comes across tiles with an on-glaze decoration that was printed and often coloured in with enamels before being fired in a muffle kiln at a low temperature. On-glaze decorations were naturally not as hard-wearing as those protected by a glaze covering, so these tiles could not be used indiscriminately.

Towards the end of the nineteenth century the advance and popularity of photography had an impact on the decoration of tiles. Several firms carried out experiments with the transfer of photographic images, but various technical difficulties made this process rather impractical and it soon went out of fashion. The few

Inlaid tiles made from plastic clay are easily recognisable because they can be up to an inch thick, are fairly heavy and often have the appearance of a sandwich in cross section. This sandwich of clay consists of a middle section of course gritty clay with two layers of finer quality clay at top and bottom. The shallow inlaid design can be clearly seen at the top of this tile.

examples of the early experiments that have survived have a special charm and often resemble contemporary postcards.

Fireplace tile with an on-glaze transfer print of a girl holding a basket within a rococo border, painted with enamels in blue, pink, green and ochre, c. 1880, no marks. *Collection: Author.*

Tile with a photographic image of the West Pier in Brighton, the photographic image has been printed on a cream-yellow ground, c. 1895, made by Maw & Co.
Courtesy: Ironbridge Gorge Museum, Telford.

DESIGN AND STYLISTIC SOURCES

There are certain principles that govern the design of all tiles, irrespective of historical period, style or subject matter. Every designer faces the same initial problem of filling the square or rectangle with lines, shapes and colours. Remembering the number of tiles that have been made since Sumerian and Egyptian times, one would think that variations would be virtually infinite, but nevertheless it is possible to detect certain principles of design that they all have in common.

A tile is often divided up geometrically before decorative motifs or figures are added. The Dutch painter frequently placed a circle centrally on his tile before painting his subject-matter inside it. This circle device was often used, for the perfect roundness of a circle within the stark form of a square immediately makes a pattern that is aesthetically satisfying.

Apart from the circle, quadrates, hexagons and octagons can be used, but in all cases it is the juxtaposition with the square that gives point to the shape within it.

Certain historical periods have a liking for particular geometrical patterns, as we can see in Gothic design, where the quatrefoil was an important motif. The geometrical sub-division of a tile is a factor overlooked by many collectors and yet is one of the fundamental elements which determine the tile's final character.

Some tiles have no apparent geometrical sub-division, such as those in the Art Nouveau manner in which the designs are placed either symmetrically or asymmetrically on the tile. The symmetrical and centrally placed motifs have a definite relationship with the edges of the tile, for the very reason that they are central, while the asymmetrical Art Nouveau design is often allowed to roam freely. The stalks and tendrils that weave their way over the surface seem

Geometrical division by means of a circle, transfer printed and handcoloured tile, no marks, c. 1880. *Collection: G. K. Beaulah.*

intended to demonstrate that the irregular shapes of nature will not always be bound by a neat geometrical order or conventional design.

Another feature that came to the fore in the second half of the nineteenth century was an incongruous over-elaboration of drawn or painted flowers and birds. These tiles almost rival oil paintings of similar subjects, stretching the limits of naturalism to such an extent that the distinction between painting and tile design becomes blurred. However, designers within the Arts and Crafts movement put design firmly back within the limits that they understood to be best suited to tiles, and representations of birds and flowers were once more simplified.

It is these uncluttered, flat designs that are best suited for the decoration of large wall areas in which each tile is linked through its pattern to the next. Corner motifs, which are a characteristic of many

Left: Geometrical division by means of a quadrate, transfer printed and hand coloured tile, no marks, c. 1885. *Collection: Author.*

Right: Geometrical division by means of an octagon, transfer printed and hand coloured tile, no marks, c. 1885. *Collection: Author.*

tiles, illustrate this point clearly.

If a wall was half-tiled, the edge of the tiled area was rounded off with border tiles. Square or rectangular, these appear in many different styles, but they are specially designed for their purpose, with a pattern that flows in only two directions, whereas that of a normal tile will expand in four directions.

As tiles form a permanent decorative surface which cannot be changed easily, the responsibility of a tile designer is perhaps greater than that of a designer for wallpaper or fabrics. Tiling was, as it still is, too expensive a building material to be subjected to fashionable whims, and although most designs are influenced by contemporary style, a well designed tile has a lasting quality that will be appreciated by more than one generation.

W. J. Furnival put it well when he remarked in his book *Leadless Decorative Tiles, Faience and Mosaic* that '. . . a decorated tile is not necessarily a decorative one; to make it decorative something more is needed, namely, preconceived arrangement, purpose, design. An indefinite purposeless pattern is hardly design, for design should consist not merely of the impress of mind on material, but a valuable enhancing impress, such only as the mind both intuitively artistic and well stored with knowledge is capable of imparting.'

The analysis of tile design is not an easy matter, for it means

Geometrical division by means of two diagonal bands, transfer printed tile, no marks, c. 1890. *Collection: Author.*

Geometrical division by means of octagons and squares forming an all-over pattern, transfer printed tile, Minton, registered 1881. *Collection: Author.*

An irregular division of a square by means of three oblongs and one square. Note the odd combination of stylised flowers and motifs with naturalistically drawn bindweed. Transfer printed and hand coloured tile, no marks, c. 1880. *Collection: Author.*

looking beyond the pretty colours and attractive lines and shapes at the principles that have governed tile design thoughout history. It means studying many tiles of different periods, comparing and contrasting them. An awareness of underlying design principles is a valuable asset in the appreciation and assessment of tiles.

Victorian and Edwardian tiles show the influence of many different styles and other historical sources. In fact the terms 'Victorian' and 'Edwardian' are in this context useful only to indicate period—Victorian: 1839–1901, and Edwardian: 1901–1909—and have very little meaning stylistically. Although, for instance, it is true that throughout this period many designs were very ornate, rich with flowers and other naturalistic motifs, there were also movements within it to show opposite characteristics. Art Nouveau in particular created stylised adaptations from nature, stressing the design quality rather than the faithful representation of natural objects.

It is possible to group the stylistic sources which influenced the design of Victorian and Edwardian tiles under six main headings: Naturalism, Classicism, Neo-Gothic, Oriental, the Arts and Crafts movement and Art Nouveau.

Two tiles showing the differences between a three dimensional naturalistic representation of a flower and a flat floral design by William De Morgan which has been carefully designed to fit the square tile in such a way that adjacent tiles can link on to it. *Left:* transfer printed and hand coloured tile, no marks, c. 1880. *Collection: Author. Right:* hand painted tile by William De Morgan, c. 1885. *Collection: G. K. Beaulah.*

A selection of moulded, printed and hand painted Victorian and Edwardian border tiles. *Collection: Author.*

Naturalistic representations such as these appealed to Victorian taste. *Left:* two tiles showing a stork, hand painted, signed W. Dixon, Minton Hollins & Co., c. 1880. *Collection: G. K. Beaulah. Top left:* tile with apples and blossom, transfer printed and hand coloured, no marks, c. 1885. *Collection: Author. Top right:* tile with pansies, transfer printed and hand coloured, no marks, c. 1885. *Collection: Author.*

Naturalism

Nature was an important source of ideas for the tile designer and, as many people do today, Victorians liked representations of flowers, birds, landscapes, scenes from literature and history—all of which were to be found on tiles of the period.

There was a new interest in nature, for Constable had opened people's eyes to the beauty of the English landscape and art critics such as Ruskin encouraged artists to study nature, and draw inspiration from it. Many parks were laid out in nineteenth century towns, bringing a touch of the countryside into the industrial cities. Naturalistic ornament on and in buildings fulfilled a similar function, with shops and public buildings displaying hand-painted scenes—for instance, the cow and sheep of butchers shops, some of which still, happily, survive.

Inside the houses, fireplaces were often surrounded with ornamental tiles that showed carefully painted, printed or embossed flowers and birds.

Tiles with Classical designs have a balanced elegance that gives them an enduring quality. Two tiles with daffodils in a Roman vase flanked by two griffons and set within an architectural frame, transfer printed and hand coloured, no marks, c. 1885. *Collection: Author.*

Left: tile with classical motifs and two winged lions, lithographic transfer, Craven Dunnill, c. 1892. *Right:* tile with scallop shell, garlands and olive branches, lithographic transfer, Craven Dunnill, c. 1892. *All tiles in the collection of the author.*

Classicism

The nineteenth century was also a period when designers often drew their inspiration from the past. Greek, Roman and Renaissance art were popular sources for design motifs, although it is difficult to trace these classical motifs to their exact source, as they were changed and adapted by the designer.

Classical designs are carefully balanced and symmetrical, ranging from very ornate to the extremely simple, and the designs usually have a central motif surrounded by secondary ones. There may be a Grecian vase surrounded by garlands of fruit and flowers, or a scallop shell with acanthus leaves or olive branches. In more complex designs winged lions, griphons and sometimes cherubs are used.

The combinations of all these motifs are infinite in number. Tiles with classical designs were printed, moulded and sometimes hand-painted, and they were very popular throughout the nineteenth century.

Neo-Gothic

The popularity of neo-Gothic architecture in Britain had a marked

Neo-Gothic tiles were made primarily for church use and are often faithful copies of medieval tiles. Glazed inlaid tile with a representation of the Virgin, Godwin, c. 1870. *Collection: G. K. Beaulah.*

influence on the production and design of tiles. The architect Pugin encouraged the revival of inlaid tiles of the medieval type, as we have seen, and there was a great variety of Gothic motifs that the designer could either copy or adapt. The basic elements were stylised leaves and flowers like the trefoil, quatrefoil and fleur-de-lis, but another typical Gothic idea is the four-tile pattern in which each tile made up a quarter of the total design.

Minton, Maw and Co. and Godwin made a large range of Neo-Gothic inlaid tiles of various shapes and sizes which could be assembled as floors or decorative wall panels. They were glazed or unglazed, according to fashion. Godwin was very successful in imitating the uneven surface of medieval tiles and his work is found in many churches of the last quarter of the century. The manufacturers also produced tiles with inlaid letters so that inscriptions could be added to large decorative panels. The majority of Neo-Gothic designs were inlaid and only a few of them appear in printed or moulded form.

Unglazed inlaid tile with stylised floral motif, no marks, c. 1880. *Collection: Author.*

Glazed inlaid tile with a stylised tree and two doves, Craven Dunnill, c. 1880. *Collection: Author.*

Oriental

During the eighteenth and nineteenth centuries an enormous interest in Chinese porcelain grew up in Europe. At first the porcelain was imported from China, but eventually European factories succeeded in making porcelain themselves, which they decorated with Chinese motifs. The influence spread to the decoration of tiles, and we find exotic birds and strangely dressed Chinamen set in Chinese-style landscapes.

At first this type of decoration was hand painted, as can be seen in some Dutch and English Delftware tiles, but in the nineteenth century it was usually transfer printed.

The Far East came closer again during the 1850s, when Japan signed trade agreements with some foreign countries, and also allowed foreigners to enter Japan for the first time. Within a very few years many Japanese goods, such as lacquer boxes, painted fans, ivory carvings, porcelain and wood-block prints, had found their way to Europe.

The simplicity and boldness of the wood-block prints had a strong influence on European art, including tile design. The Japanese had a particular liking for branches with blossom, the rising sun and chrysanthemums (this flower was first used as a design motif in China and was later taken up by Japan, where it became a symbol of Japanese imperial power).

Tiles based on Chinese and Japanese designs were very popular in the 19th century. *Above:* tile with Japanese landscape, transfer printed, Copeland, c. 1875. *Top far left:* tile with bamboo design, transfer printed and hand coloured, no marks, c. 1885. *Near left:* tile with branches, transfer printed, Minton, c. 1885. *All tiles in the collection of the author.*

The Arts and Crafts Movement

Dissatisfaction with the aesthetic qualities of the manufactured goods shown at the Great Exhibition at the Crystal Palace in 1851 was one of the main drives behind the formation of the Arts and Crafts movement in the second half of the nineteenth century. William Morris was the organising force behind the movement, together with such men as Walter Crane, C. A. Voysey and William De Morgan. They opposed the use of the machine where it led to the debasement of the craftsman's work and eliminated the joy of making things by hand.

William Morris and his followers turned their backs on the machine and produced only hand made articles, which they wanted to be available to everybody: in the event, because so few were produced they were expensive, and could be afforded only by the rich aesthetes of the day.

William De Morgan was a prolific designer of tiles and his work shows great feeling for line and form. But if these hand made tiles could not be bought by many people, they did influence the design of many of the mass produced tiles. The work done by this group of designers in the field of fabrics, wallpaper and decorative metalwork all has a distinctive quality, the designs being often flat, or nearly so, with a certain amount of stylisation which proved better suited to tiles than the elaborate three-dimensional flowers and scrolls of many Victorian designers.

The Arts and Crafts designer looked to examples from Japan and Persia, of which simplicity and sensitivity of line and form are the

Tiles inspired by the Arts and Crafts movement have strong design qualities. *Far left:* tile with large sunflower, transfer printed and hand coloured, Sherwin & Cotton, registered in 1881. *Near left:* tile with sunflower and intersecting bands, transfer printed and hand coloured, no marks, c. 1880. *Above:* tile with stylised flowers, lithographic transfer, Craven Dunnill, 1892. *All tiles in the collection of the author.*

hallmarks. In the field of tiles the Persians had developed great technical skill and a high degree of decorative expertise, and William De Morgan especially studied these examples.

Printing is the method most sympathetic to this type of work, in particular lithographic printing, which will print flat areas of colour with a boldness not easily achieved with prints taken from etched or engraved plates.

Art Nouveau tiles are much sought after by collectors because of their elegant designs and attractive colours.

Left: tile with clover leaves in relief, transucent glaze, no marks, c. 1905.

Right: tile with stylised flower and leaves in relief, translucent glazes, no marks, c. 1900. *Both tiles in the collection of the author.*

Art Nouveau

Art Nouveau is the name of an art movement that swept through Europe at the end of the nineteenth century and the beginning of the twentieth. Based on designs that were adaptations from nature, normally flowers and plants, the main characteristic of Art Nouveau is the restless and sinuous line.

The chief exponents of this art form in Britain—where it never became as extreme as on the Continent—were the illustrator Aubrey Beardsley, the architect and designer Arthur Mackmurdo and the silversmith Archibald Knox. Scotland had its own branch of Art Nouveau in Charles Rennie Mackintosh, the Macdonald sisters and Herbert MacNair, who were known as the 'Glasgow Four'. Liberty's in London did a great deal to popularise the new style and sold many of its products, from fabrics to glass lampshades.

The fashion spread to the decoration of tiles, which showed the typical characteristics of delicate and graceful lines, using relief patterns that simulated the technique of tube-lining. The areas between the raised lines were filled with the richly coloured majolica glazes that make these tiles so attractive.

Art Nouveau was primarily suited to the applied arts, and because it lacked proper roots in architecture and painting it was short lived: it had come to a virtual end by 1910.

Top left: tile with stylised tulip in relief, translucent glazes, no marks, c. 1905. *Top right:* tile with two stylised flowers in relief, translucent glazes, no marks, c. 1900. *Bottom left:* tile with swirling convolvulus in relief, translucent glazes, no marks, c. 1900. *Bottom right:* tile with a design based on a water lily, translucent glazes, no marks, c. 1905. *All tiles in the collection of the author.*

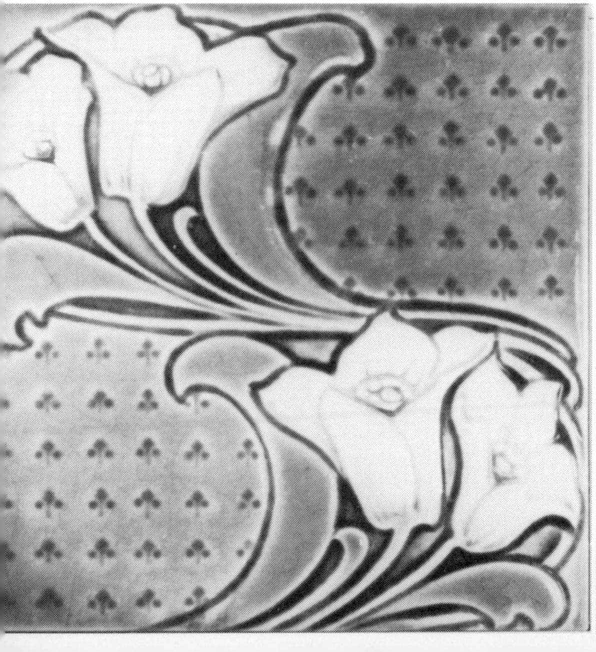

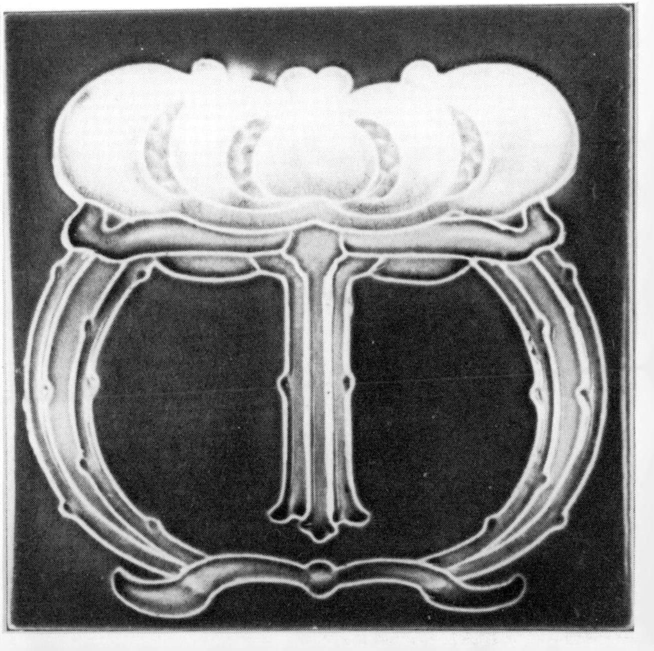

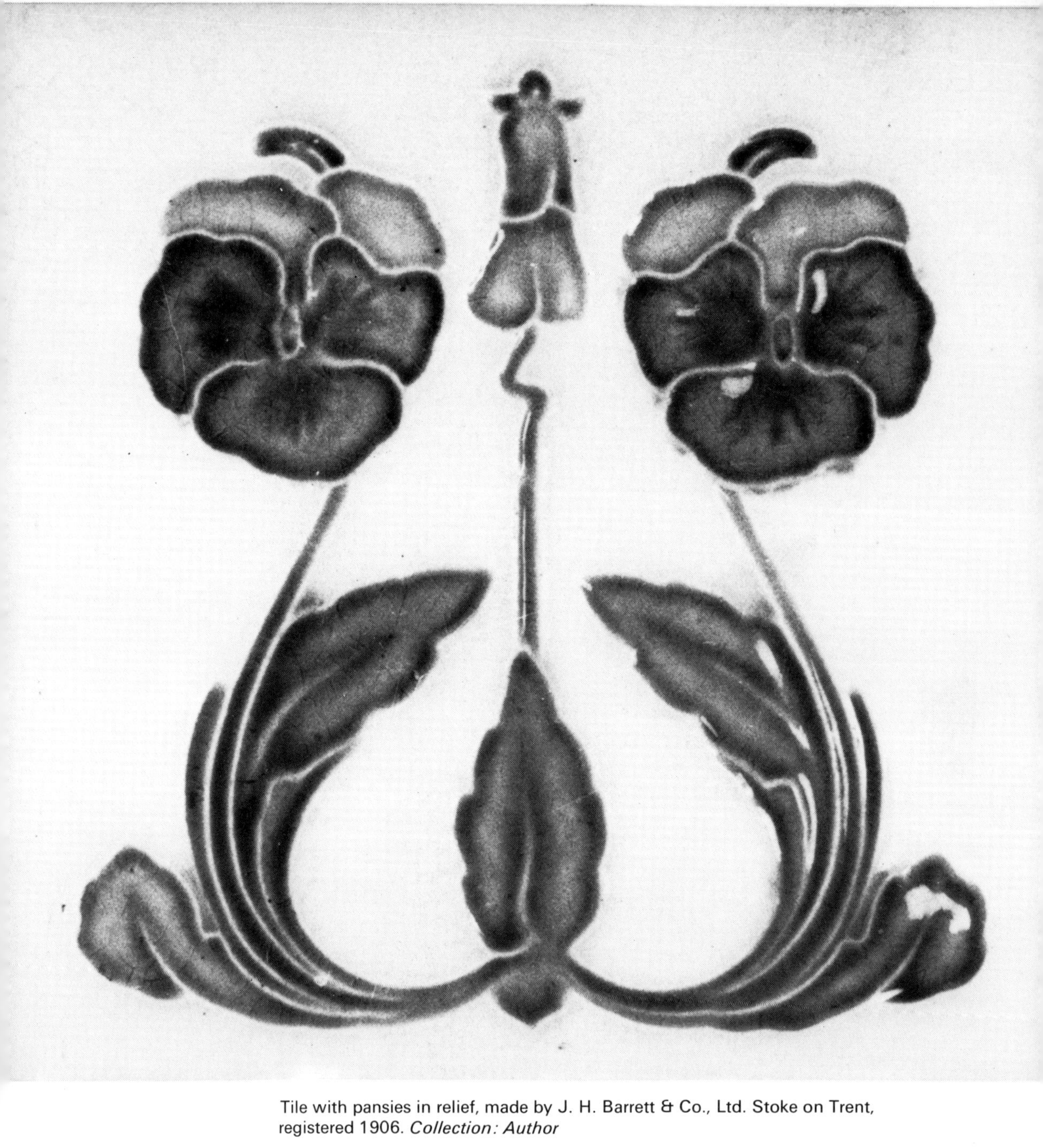

Tile with pansies in relief, made by J. H. Barrett & Co., Ltd. Stoke on Trent, registered 1906. *Collection: Author*

During the 1920s and 30s tile designs often became abstract *Right:* border tile with a geometrical pattern of raised lines, translucent glazes, H. & R. Johnson, c. 1925. *Below:* tile with pattern of nail heads and extended nail heads in relief, translucent glaze, H. & R. Johnson, c. 1920. *Tiles in the collection of the author.*

During the 1920s and thirties, abstract art and the use of elementary form in architecture had begun to affect Britain from the Continent. Pictorial representation on tiles became less common and in certain cases began to be replaced by the abstract geometrical pattern of Art Deco. Some Art Deco tiles of the period show the imaginative use of basic forms, but in many instances all use of form was abandoned and the tile was decorated instead with marble-textured glazes, which became popular for tile fireplaces. Tiles were also coated with plain eggshell glazes to emphasise the smooth surface texture.

THEMES AND SUBJECTS ON VICTORIAN TILES

The great variety of Victorian subject-matter gives the collector an opportunity to specialise in certain themes. You can find tiles showing flowers, birds, animals, landscapes, scenes from literature and mythology, portraits and scenes from children's stories. Tiles decorated with flowers and birds are more common than those illustrating scenes from literature or portraits, so it goes without saying that the latter are more sought after and expensive.

Plants and flowers provided the designer with an endless source of shapes, lines and colours, and of all motifs were the most frequently used. They were shown naturalistically, as many Victorians preferred, or in more stylised and abstract forms, as in the tiles produced by the Arts and Crafts movements and Art Nouveau.

The many printed or painted flowers, although recognisable as certain species—such as roses or lilies—are not necessarily accurate

Flowers always have been and always will be a popular subject matter and their beauty has been captured on many Victorian tiles. *Left:* tile with spray of azaleas, transfer printed and hand-coloured. Decorative Art Tile C. Ltd., registered in 1889. *Right:* tile with large chrysanthemum, transfer printed and hand-coloured, no marks, c. 1885. *Both tiles in the collection of the author.*

Left: tile with a sunflower, transfer printed, no marks, c. 1890.

Right: tile with a lily, transfer printed and hand coloured, no marks, c. 1885. *Both tiles in the collection of the author.*

from a botanical standpoint, and sometimes it can be very difficult to identify a certain flower.

During the 1870s and eighties there was a change in the fashion of garden design, with a return to the simple formality of late seventeenth-century gardens: neatly clipped hedges and such 'old fashioned' flowers as lilies, poppies, hollyhocks, sunflowers and roses. This type of garden inspired painters, poets and designers alike, and you will find the flowers both in Pre-Raphaelite paintings and in the poetry of Tennyson . . .

There has fallen a splendid tear
From the passion-flower at the gate.
She is coming, my dove, my dear;
She is coming, my life, my fate;
The red rose cries, 'She is near, she is near;'
And the white rose weeps, 'She is late;'
The larkspur listens, 'I hear, I hear;'
And the lily whispers, 'I wait.'

Floral tiles of that period reflect this interest, and the sunflower and lily in particular are often represented.

Fruit of various kinds appears on many tiles in printed, painted or moulded form. Brambles, apples, peaches, pears, strawberries, tomatoes and pomegranates are all quite common.

Above: tile with wild roses, transfer printed and hand coloured, no marks, c. 1880.

Right: moulded tile with roses, Sherwin & Cotton, c. 1885. *Both tiles in the collection of the Author.*

There are many different kinds of fruit depicted on both Victorian and Art Nouveau tiles. *Left:* tile with strawberries, transfer printed and hand coloured, registered in 1891.

Right: tile with tomatoes stamped in relief, translucent glaze, c. 1900. *Both tiles in the collection of the author.*

Some fruits were regarded as having special symbolic significance—tomatoes, which used to be called 'love apples', or pomegranates, are symbols of fertility or of resurrection, while the apple can symbolise temptation, and the bramble, neglect. Pre-Raphaelite painters often used fruit to emphasise the 'message' of their work; there is a bitten apple on the lap of the temptress in Holman Hunt's *Hireling Shepherd* and D. G. Rossetti's *Pro perina* is holding a pomegranate.

Pictures telling a story were popular with the Victorians and several firms produced tiles with scenes from literature, drama or the Bible. From Minton, for example, came scenes in sets of twelve, with stories from the Old and New Testaments, Shakespeare and the Medieval Romances most in demand. Moyr Smith, a designer for Minton, created many of these picture tiles. They were invariably printed lithographically in one or more colours.

Portraits of the great and famous were also popular in pre-television days. Queen Victoria and Prince Albert were probably the two personalities most often portrayed on tiles and other ceramics, and manufacturers would sometimes issue a series of portraits on such occasions as the Queen's jubilee.

We also find portraits of great statesmen such as Gladstone or Lord Salisbury, victorious soldiers such as Baden Powell, and popular heroines such as Florence Nightingale.

These portraits were reproduced using a variety of techniques which included printing and relief. Of course, portrait tiles are now of great historical interest and can be relatively expensive, but a determined collector will come across them occasionally and if they are in good condition they are certainly worth buying both for interest and for investment.

Like fruit and flowers, birds have a strong visual appeal in their varied shapes and colours whether they are represented naturalistically or in a more stylised form—especially if they are part of a decorative scheme. Peacocks, kingfishers and swans are found frequently on tiles and the designer William De Morgan often introduced exotic species such as the ostrich or the extinct dodo into his designs.

From the animal world, rabbits, cows, sheep, fish and even frogs made their appearance. The influence of the Dutch and English animal painters is easily detected; a few cows under a tree in a rustic landscape is reminiscent of the seventeenth-century Dutch painter Paulus Potter, while deer and dogs were the speciality of the Victorian painter Landseer. Minton produced a series of tiles illustrating animal fables to appeal to children.

English water colourists of the eighteenth and nineteenth

The many birds found on Victorian tiles could fill an aviary. They come in all shapes and colours. *Left:* tile showing a blue tit near a nest, transfer printed and signed L. T. Swetnam, Minton, c. 1890. *Collection: Author. Right:* tile with two birds on a branch, transfer printed, no marks, c. 1890. *Collection: J. Rumsby.*

Quiet pastoral scenes with animals are delightful and popular with collectors. *Left:* tile showing a stag and his does, designed by William Wise, transfer printed, Minton, c. 1885. *Courtesy: Minton Museum, Royal Doulton Tableware Ltd.*

Right: tile with a bull and a cow under a tree designed by William Wise, transfer printed, Minton, c. 1885. *Courtesy: Gladstone Pottery Museum, Stoke-on-Trent.*

Above: tile with a hand-painted scene of Ullswater, over-glaze enamels, Maw & Co., c. 1880. *Collection: G. K. Beaulah.*

Imaginary landscapes and actual beauty spots were depicted on tiles. *Right*: tile showing a windmill, transfer printed, Minton, c. 1885. *Collection: Author.*

Shakespeare was a source of inspiration for many Victorian tile designers, as can be seen in these two tiles. *Left:* tile with a scene from King Lear, designed by Moyr Smith, lithographic transfer, Minton, c. 1885. *Collection: Author.*
Right: tile with a scene from Romeo and Juliet, lithographic transfer, E. Smith & Co., c. 1885. *Collection: G. K. Beaulah.*

centuries had also created a fashion for scenes of far-way places—romantic landscapes with trees and ruins. Landscapes on tiles can be clumsy, as their perspective and scale are not always accurate, but this can add to their charm. Landscape tiles were hand painted or transfer printed, and sometimes even made in relief.

Printed or painted pastoral scenes on Victorian tiles were relics of the eighteenth century, when there was a great interest among the urban wealthy in the ideal of a simple country life. Idyllic scenes with shepherds, nymphs and milkmaids were popular in an age when classical literature formed an important part of education. The pastoral life was often pictured in paintings and engravings, and eventually on tiles as well.

Another interesting theme was the personification—usually in the form of a woman—of the seasons and elements. 'Air' was shown as a woman floating in the air among birds and butterflies; 'Water' puts her among the water lilies; in 'Earth' she is among fruit and flowers, and for 'Fire' she is holding a torch or bending over a fire. Other subjects were 'Sports' and 'Hospitality'.

Portrait tiles never fail to fascinate as is the case with the two examples chosen here. *Left:* tile with a portrait of Lord Salisbury, stamped in relief, translucent glaze, J. Edwards, 1897.

This thematic type of design appeared usually on the better quality tiles, which were often used for a fireplace or entrance porch. Some fine hand made and hand decorated examples were produced by Burmantofts.

Pictures from children's stories and nursery rhymes, on tiles intended for the nursery, followed the styles and fashions of the Victorian illustrators of children's books—Walter Crane, Kate Greenaway and Randolph Caldecott. In fact, Walter Crane himself designed some tiles for Maw and Co.

Nursery tiles range from finely executed etchings and engravings to bold outline drawings with flat colours which show the influence of Japanese wood-block prints. Like portrait tiles, those with children's illustrations add to the value of your collection.

Right: tile with a portrait of Queen Victoria, stamped in relief, translucent glaze, J. Edwards, 1897. *Both tiles in the collection of the author.*

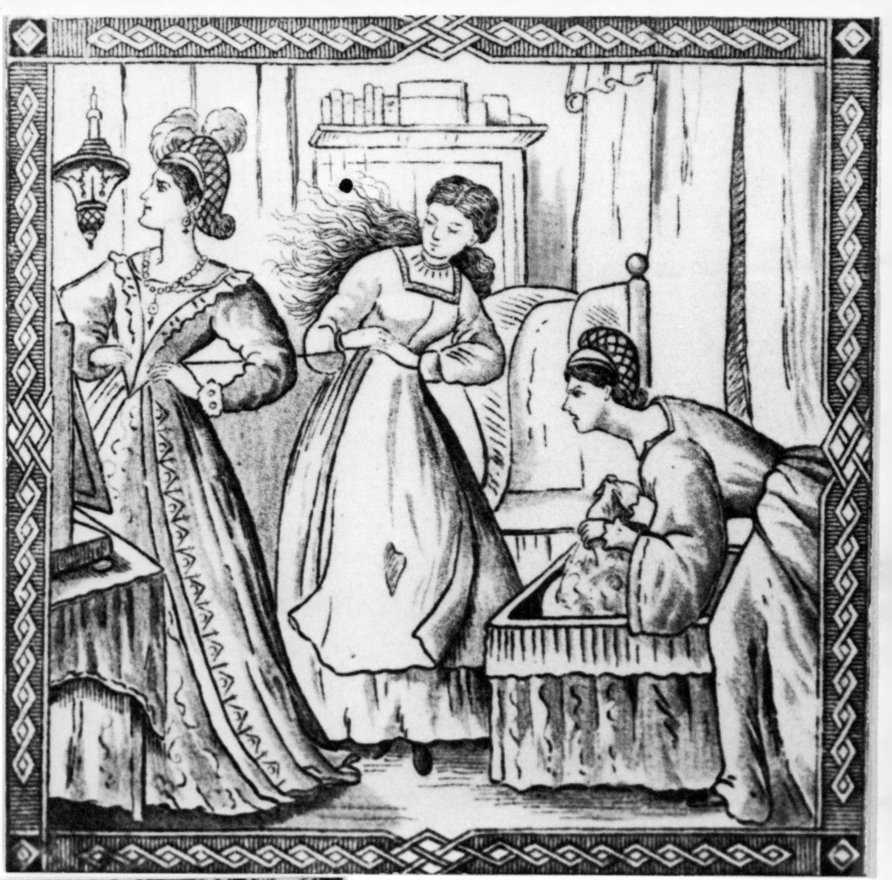

Tiles with children's illustrations have become coveted items among collectors. Tile with a scene from Cinderella, transfer printed, no marks, c. 1885. *Gladstone Pottery Museum, Stoke-on-Trent.*

Tile with illustrations for children, transfer printed, Minton, Hollins & Co., c. 1885. *Collection: Author.*

Shepherds and milkmaids in pastoral settings make charming tile decorations. *Left:* tile with a shepherd and his dog watching over their flock, transfer printed, Minton, c. 1880. *Right:* tile showing a milkmaid crossing a brook, transfer printed, Minton, c. 1880. *Both tiles in the collection of G. K. Beaulah.*

Tile measuring 6″ × 2″ showing a shepherdess crossing a stream, executed in relief, Sharwin & Cotton, c. 1885. *Collection: Author.*

The personification of the seasons and the elements is a fascinating subject matter. *Left:* tiles with flowers and plants symbolising the seasons, transfer printed, no marks, c. 1885.

Right: tile with the personification of the elements, transfer printed, E. Smith & Co., c. 1885. *Both tiles in the collection of G. K. Beaulah.*

FAMOUS TILE MANUFACTURERS AND DESIGNERS

The firm of Minton is now something of a legend in the history of nineteenth-century tiles. The company was started by Thomas Minton in Stoke-on-Trent in 1793 and was well established when his son Herbert took control in 1836 and proceeded to lay the foundation of the nineteenth-century British tile industry.

In 1830 Samuel Wright of Shelton had taken out a patent for the manufacture of inlaid tiles but after some unsuccessful attempts to produce them on a commercial basis he sold his patent to Herbert Minton who was greatly interested in tiles of medieval date. After several experiments he began to make reproductions of medieval examples and in 1842 he brought out a catalogue called *Examples of Old English Tiles*, which showed replicas he had made of floor tiles in the Chapter House of Westminster Abbey. These tiles proved popular with Gothic Revival architects and by the 1850s the firm was well known for its inlaid reproductions. They were used not only in churches but also in town halls, museums, libraries and private homes.

Herbert Minton also took advantage of a clay dust-pressing process invented by Prosser in 1840 and adapted it to the production of tiles after buying a share of the patent. In 1845 he went into partnership with Michael Daintry Hollins, Mrs. Minton's nephew, and it would seem that the tile making section of the firm became a separate concern under the name Minton, Hollins and Co.

In 1848 Herbert Minton joined printers from London, Messrs. Collins and Reynolds, in taking out a patent for a type of lithographic printing by which impressions were taken from a flat stone and then transferred to pottery, and after some initial difficulties this method of printing flat colours proved to be very successful for printing on tiles. One of the partnership's first commissions for this type of tile

Tiles made by Mintons China Works are keenly collected by many tile enthusiasts. The tiles range from inlaid tiles to hand painted and printed tiles. *Top left:* lithographically printed tile, c. 1880. *Top right:* lithographically printed border tile, c. 1885. *Collection: Author. Bottom right:* a round inlaid tile with a Minton date mark of 1864. *Collection: G. K. Beaulah.*

was for the smoking room of the Palace of Westminster, using designs by A. W. N. Pugin. In 1849 Colin Minton Campbell joined the firm, and when Herbert Minton died in 1858 the company was continued by Messrs. Hollins and Campbell.

This partnership ended in 1868 but Michael Hollins continued the manufacture of tiles under the name Minton, Hollins & Co., while the parent company of Minton also continued to make tiles—which were stamped 'Mintons China Works'. During the second half of the nineteenth century both companies produced a large range of tiles which were hand painted or printed, and pressed in relief.

In 1867 Minton, Hollins and Co. received a commission to make majolica tiles for the Gamble room in the Victoria and Albert Museum, which was then being built. This room still counts as one of the prime examples of the use of ceramic tiles in the decoration of a building, combining as it does function with beauty.

From the middle of the nineteenth century several tile manufacturers began to follow closely in the footsteps of Minton. The most successful of these was Maw and Co., started by the brothers George

Minton, Hollins & Co., although a separate firm, produced tiles like Mintons China Works. *Right:* moulded tile, translucent glazes, c. 1880. *Collection: Author.*

Maw & Co. produced excellent quality tiles of which some are illustrated here. *Top left:* glazed encaustic tile, c. 1870. *Collection C. Hammond. Top right:* transfer printed tile, c. 1870. *Collection: J. Rumsby. Bottom left:* lithographically printed tile, c. 1890. *Collection: Author.*

Wedgwood produced an interesting range of picture tiles which are now much sought after. Transfer printed tile representing the month of June, c. 1885. *Collection: Author.*

and Arthur Maw in 1850 when they bought the stocks of the Barr and St. John encaustic tile works in Worcester. In 1852 they moved to Broseley where they started the Benthal Works not far from Ironbridge and soon began to rival Minton with their output of inlaid tiles. M. D. Wyatt was one of their designers, and it was he who designed the pictorial pavement 'The Seasons', made of mosaic and inlaid tiles, which was shown at the International Exhibition of 1862.

Maw and Co. also began the production of wall tiles using a variety of techniques, and rivalled Minton's production of majolica. Between 1887 and 1906 they employed Charles Temple, who was a prolific designer of single tiles as well as of large pictorial compositions. In 1883 a new Benthal Works was built near the river, in Jackfield, and there the firm carried on until the late 1960s when the premises, together with a priceless stock of old tiles and plaster

Transfer printed tile showing the Nativity, Wedgwood, c. 1885. *Collection: G. K. Beaulah.*

Transfer printed tile representing the month of July, Wedgwood, c. 1885. *Collection: G. K. Beaulah.*

moulds, were acquired by the Ironbridge Gorge Museum.

Also in Jackfield, not far from Maw's factory at Benthall, there still stands the factory which was used by Craven Dunnill. They, like Maw's, competed with Minton with their range of inlaid, printed and majolica tiles and they were also noted for the quality of their plain tiles. Craven Dunnill occupied the site of previous potteries and it was here that Peter Stephan tried his hand at making inlaid tiles at the beginning of the nineteenth century, his trade-mark being an anchor and a cable. Craven Dunnill was active between 1872 and 1951.

The celebrated firm of Wedgwood produced some tiles between 1870 and 1900. Their tiles are sought by collectors, primarily for their name, but also because they often depict scenes of great charm. They produced sets of transfer printed tiles with themes such as Robin Hood, A Midsummer Night's Dream and Little Red Riding

Burmantofts produced charming hand made tiles of which this tile showing putti playing with a goat is a good example. The tile is executed in relief and has a translucent glaze.

William De Morgan's tiles are in a class of their own, difficult to obtain but when available worth every penny. Tile with hand painted Persian design in blue, green and black, Chelsea period. *Gladstone Pottery Museum, Stoke-on-Trent.*

Hood, while tiles with photographic views of American monuments and sailing ships were also a speciality.

In the south of England, at Poole in Dorset, Jesse Carter founded the firm of Carter and Co. in 1873. By the 1890s they had a considerable reputation for the production of tiles and faience and in 1895 took over the Architectural Pottery at Hamworthy, Poole, greatly increasing their business. They produced some interesting tiles as late as the 1920s and thirties which were often hand painted.

Two of their most productive designers at that time were Harold Stabler and Dora Batty, who designed tiles with birds, nursery rhymes and nursery toys. Harold Stabler also did some tiles for the London Transport Passenger Board in 1939.

During the 1880s Burmantoft's in Leeds produced some very fine hand made tiles decorated with flowers painted with slip and coloured glazes and animals executed in relief. Burmantoft's was owned by Wilcock and Co., who were taken over by Leeds Fireclay in 1889. They continued the art pottery side of the firm until 1904.

During the tile boom in the second half of the nineteenth century many other companies took advantage of the increased demand. Some of the most notable were W. T. Copeland and Sons, Stoke-on-Trent; T. and R. Boote Ltd., Waterloo Pottery, Burslem; Malkin Edge and Co., Burslem; and Sherwin and Cotton, Hanley. The beginning of the twentieth century saw the establishment of Pilkington's Tile and Pottery Co. Ltd., Manchester, together with H. and R. Johnson Ltd., Cobridge, who are both major tile manufacturers at present.

Tile manufacturers employed specialist designers for the decoration of their wares, although the results can range from mere hackwork to designs with undeniable aesthetic qualities. Most designers were professionally trained artists who were either employed full time by certain firms or pursued their own careers as designers, painters or architects while doing occasional work for

Tile with hand painted Persian design in blue, green, yellow and purple, William De Morgan, Chelsea period. *Gladstone Pottery Museum, Stoke-on-Trent.*

The John Taylor Teachers' Centre in Headingley, Leeds has five fireplaces with tiles made by William De Morgan of which a detail is shown here. Tile with a sea horse in ruby lustre, Chelsea period.

Two tiles with sailing boats painted in green, William De Morgan, Chelsea period. The John Taylor Teachers' Centre in Headingley. *Courtesy Leeds Education Authority.*

The prolific draughtsmanship of Moyr Smith makes his tiles an attractive asset to every collection. *Left:* tile showing King Alfred and his court lithographic transfer print, Minton, c. 1885. *Collection J. Rumsby. Right:* tile with a scene from Shakespeare's *Cymbeline*, lithographic transfer print, Minton, c. 1885. *Collection: Author.*

such firms as Minton, Maw and Co., and Wedgwood.

The majority of Victorian tiles were designed by anonymous artists drawing inspiration from standard text books on design such as Owen Jones' well known *Grammar of Ornament* and Glazier's *Manual of Historic Ornament*, but there were also very original designers like William De Morgan and Moyr Smith who formulated their own easily recognisable style.

William De Morgan is an unusual figure; he was not only a prolific designer, but was also interested in the technical aspects of tile making. He involved himself in the chemistry of ceramic colours, and the use of lustre became one of his specialities. He was closely associated with William Morris and his circle and like them wanted to raise the quality of design. He made a study of Persian design and ceramics and was also influenced by the many products imported from Japan. His tile designs exhibit considerable aesthetic quality, with a strong feeling for line and form, and at times, too, a sense of humour enlivens his work.

Between 1872 and 1882 De Morgan lived at Cheyne Row, Chelsea,

A page from Moyr Smith's *Album of Decorative Figures*, published in London in 1882, with designs for the Tennyson tiles. *Courtesy: Abbey House Museum, Leeds.*

where he started his pottery career with a few kilns at the bottom of his garden. It was here that he produced his first tiles and other ceramic ware and created most of his designs.

The subject matter of his tiles falls into three categories: animals, flowers and ships. The variety of his animal designs could fill a small zoo with species like rabbits, horses, snakes, fishes, frogs, lions, peacocks, eagles, storks, pelicans, and dodos, and others that are entirely the products of his imagination. His flower designs are usually based on roses and carnations but sometimes also on Persian floral motifs, and his designs for sailing ships were popular with buyers throughout his pottery career.

All his tiles were hand painted and he employed assistants who worked under his close supervision. He would produce a master design to be copied by the assistant, and to ensure close adherence to the original a piece of glass was placed over the original design and the assistant placed a very thin piece of paper on the glass and traced the master design with ceramic colour. This paper was then put on the already slipcoated and transparent glaze dusted tile. During the firing the paper disappeared leaving the design on the tile.

Many of De Morgan's tiles were executed in lustre and he experimented for many years with this difficult technique, perfecting it and trying to achieve various colours. Lustre is obtained by painting a compound containing metallic oxide on to the surface of the tile and at a certain critical stage during the firing, smoke is introduced into the kiln, and this changes the oxide into a thin film of metal. Ruby lustre is derived from copper and yellow lustre from silver. A good lustre tile produces beautiful colour effects when seen in the right light.

It is instructive to contrast Moyr Smith as designer with William De Morgan. Smith's designs were reproduced mechanically on tiles in large numbers, and unlike De Morgan he did not involve himself personally with the production of tiles. His work ranges from designs for tiles and plaques, to cartoons for stained glass and large pictorial panels. He worked for Minton between 1882 and 1889, but also made some tile designs for W. B. Simpson and Sons, London, and at times undertook special commissions like the pictorial friezes in the recreation hall at the sanatorium, Virginia Water.

Among tile collectors, Moyr Smith is best known for his many

William Wise, who designed tiles for Mintons China Works between 1878 and 1885, was a competent draughtsman. *Left:* One of William Wise's sketches for a tile. This drawing would be engraved into a copper-plate from which prints were transferred to tiles. *Right:* The actual tile. *Courtesy: Minton Museum, Royal Doulton Tableware Ltd., Stoke-on-Trent.*

tiles showing scenes from English literature which were manufactured by Minton. His figures show the influence of Greece and the Renaissance. Each set usually contains twelve tiles, of which the following are best known: the Waverley tiles with scenes from Sir Walter Scott's novels; the Tennyson tiles based on the *Idylls of the King*; the Thomson tiles taken from Thomson's poem *The Seasons*; the Anacreon tiles with figures in Greek costumes representing guests at an Argive feast; the Trade tiles showing various occupations; scenes from the Old and the New Testaments, and Aesop's fables.

All his figures have a distinct quality of strong but elegant line drawn with great skill, and are well adapted to the lithographic printing process used. They appear in a variety of colours and are usually signed either with his full name or his initials.

The book illustrator Walter Crane worked at times for Maw and Co., Wedgwood, Minton and Pilkington. His designs are characterised by simple outlines and flat colours. Sir Henry Cole, W. S. Coleman, William Wise, Christopher Dresser and C. A. Voysey may be cited among other distinguished designers who turned their attention to tiles in the nineteenth century.

AMERICAN TILES

Until the second half of the nineteenth century there were no tile manufacturers in America and all tiles used there had to be imported from Europe—during the eighteenth century, from England and Holland. Later, in the 1850s and sixties, such firms as Minton dominated the American market, an example being the Minton floor tiles in the Capitol. However, at that time the first steps in the production of floor tiles were already being taken in the United States, often by men who had come from England with experience of English potteries.

In 1853 the United States Pottery in Bennington made some inlaid tiles which were used to cover a floor area for exhibits at the Crystal Palace Exhibition in New York. Ten inches (25 cm) square, they had an ornamental design in the centre with an American flag in each corner.

Before 1872 Messrs. Hyzer and Lewellen of Philadelphia were experimenting with the production of floor tiles using plastic clay, but a few years later the dust-pressing process was introduced, and by the middle of the 1870s several firms, such as the American Encaustic Tiling Co. and the Star Encaustic Tile Company, had begun producing floor tiles.

Home-produced glazed relief tiles, of which those made by the Low Art Tile Company are outstanding examples, came on the market at the end of the 1870s. Now the first American tile firms began to compete successfully with their English counterparts, although, unlike the well established English firms such as Minton, Maw and Wedgwood, the American companies were often short lived. The Low Art Tile Company, for instance, was quite successful with its often highly-commended relief tiles, yet it managed to stay in business for only sixteen years.

A page from a catalogue of art tiles made by J. G. & J. F. Low. It shows a good selection of tiles pressed in relief with a choice of portraits, classical motifs and abstract patterns. *Courtesy: Hanley Central Library, Stoke-on-Trent.*

A delightful tile with dancing frogs executed in relief and covered with pink translucent glaze and was made by the American Encaustic Tiling Co. c. 1900. Cincinnati Art Museum, Ohio (*Gift of T. A. Langstroth*).

The company was established in 1877 in Chelsea, Massachusetts, by John G. Low, who pioneered the production of a type of relief tile that he called 'natural tiles'. His novel technique enabled him to fix impressions of natural objects like plants and grasses by simply placing them on the surface of an unfired tile and forcing them into the clay with a screw press so that when the leaf was removed an exact impression was left on the tile in intaglio. A thin piece of paper was then placed over the impression and some dust clay placed on top of the paper and pressed in a screw press using the first tile as a mould; when the two tiles were separated and the paper removed, the second tile carried the leaf's shape in raised relief.

The tile was then dried, fired and glazed with a transparent glaze, usually of one colour. The effect thus achieved formed a new departure from the familiar printed, painted and relief tiles of many English firms, and Low's tiles attracted a great deal of attention at an exhibition in Crewe in England, where they competed with the most famous firms of the United Kingdom.

The exhibition at Crewe opened on September 2nd 1880, and the following day the firm received a cablegram saying: 'Low won Gold Medal'. This achievement was recalled in 1895 by the American C. T. Davis in his book *A Practical Treatise on the Manufacture of Brick, Tiles and Terra-Cotta* where he writes: 'The development of tile making in the United States has been the most remarkable instance of rapid progress of an industry of any country or age, and our tile makers may be relied upon to hold the place they have gained against all the competition of Europe'.

The Low Art Tile Company's relief tiles were made from plastic clay as well as by means of the dust-pressing process, and apart from

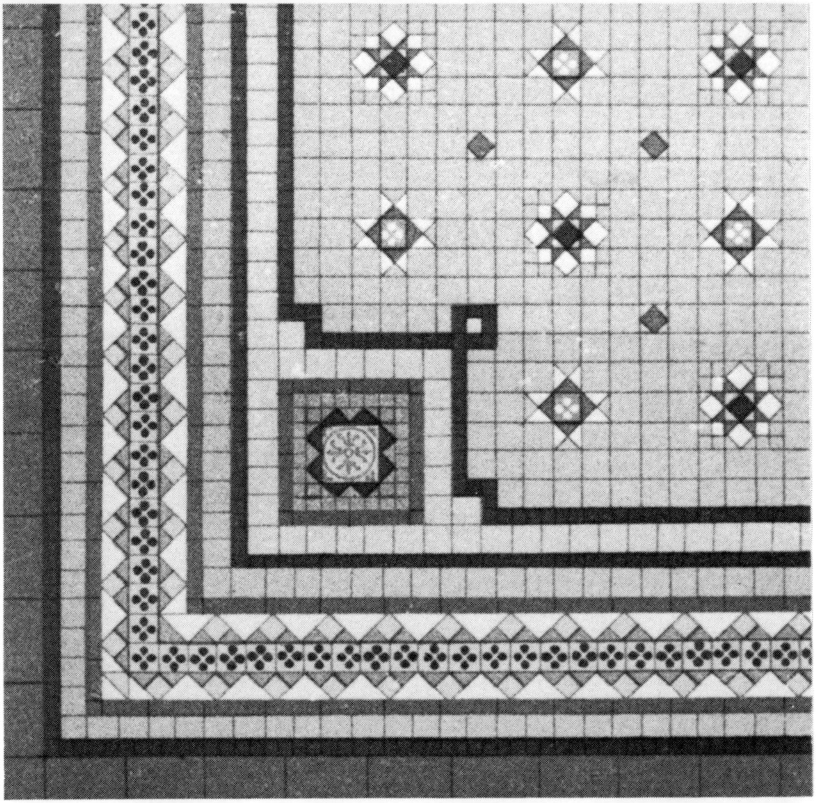

Two examples of mosaic floors with plain and inlaid tiles made by the Star Encaustic Tile Company. Small tiles of many different shapes and colours were assembled to form magnificent floors like these.

A drawing of the Rookwood Pottery in Cincinnati. The chimneys of the three bottle kilns can be seen sticking through the roof. *Courtesy: Leeds Central Library.*

their 'natural tiles' they also produced a large range of more conventional relief tiles showing portraits, abstract patterns and classical motifs.

One of their outstanding designers was Arthur Osborne, who was associated with the firm from the very beginning and designed many of their tiles. His relief tiles are sometimes referred to as 'plastic sketches'. He produced the master tile design from which casts were made, and these were used to make tiles in screw presses. In certain instances high relief tiles could be undercut by hand after having been formed in a screw press.

Low's tiles were used for fireplace surrounds, stoves, panels and soda fountains. In 1883 John Low retired from the firm and his son, John F. Low, became associated with his father under the name J. G. and J. F. Low. The firm continued until 1893.

The American Encaustic Tiling Co. began business in Zanesville, Ohio, in 1875. The everyday running of the company was the responsibility of G. A. Stanbery who, with the financial aid of Mr. B. Fischer the company president, made the firm a strong competitor in the field of American tiles, producing both inlaid and glazed relief tiles. The majority of their relief tiles were designed by Herman Mueller, a German immigrant who had studied at the Art Academy of Munich.

One of the company's more unusual techniques was the

Mary Louise McLaughlin was one of the outstanding pottery decorators of her day in Cincinnati. *Courtesy: Leeds Central Library.*

production of tiles with portraits in relief which when glazed had a surface giving the appearance of photographs. The secret consisted in modelling the portrait and covering it with black translucent glaze, so that the varying thicknesses of the glaze produced gradations of tone ranging from black and grey to almost white.

By 1892 the firm had thirty-nine kilns in operation covering a thirty-five acre site on the western bank of the Muskingum river.

The Star Encaustic Tile Company started operating in Pittsburg, Pennsylvania, in 1876 under the energetic management of Samuel Keys, who was born in Derby in 1832 and emigrated to America in 1862. The speciality of the firm was the production of a large range of mosaic and inlaid tiles for geometric pavements. Like many other American tile companies they used natural gas to fire their kilns.

The Trent Tile Company, Trenton, New Jersey, was formed in 1882. They pioneered a matt-finished tile by sand blasting their relief tiles after glazing. In 1886 they employed William Wood Gallimore as their designer and he proved to be a prolific artist, despite having only one arm. His career began in Burslem, Staffordshire, where he studied part-time at the art school of Stoke-on-Trent while being employed in the office of a solicitor. His work attracted the attention of a Mr. G. Reade, designer and modeller, who gave him a position in his studio in Burslem. Here Gallimore learned the intricacies of the trade, and after Reade's retirement he continued his studies under the Frenchman, Louis Kremer. While still in England Gallimore made some busts of prominent Englishmen, including a portrait of Llewellyn Jewitt, the author of *Ceramic Art of Great Britain*.

During his employment at the Trent Tile Company he executed most of their tile designs. Classical motifs, such as cupids engaging in various sports, rate among his best work.

Cincinnati occupies an important place in the history of American ceramics, including tiles, for the outstanding quality of the work produced there.

E. A. Barber says in his book *The Pottery and Porcelain of the United States*: 'It is safe to assert that no ceramic establishment which has existed in the United States has come nearer fulfilling the requirements of a distinctly American institution than the Rookwood Pottery of Cincinnati, Ohio. For this reason, and because

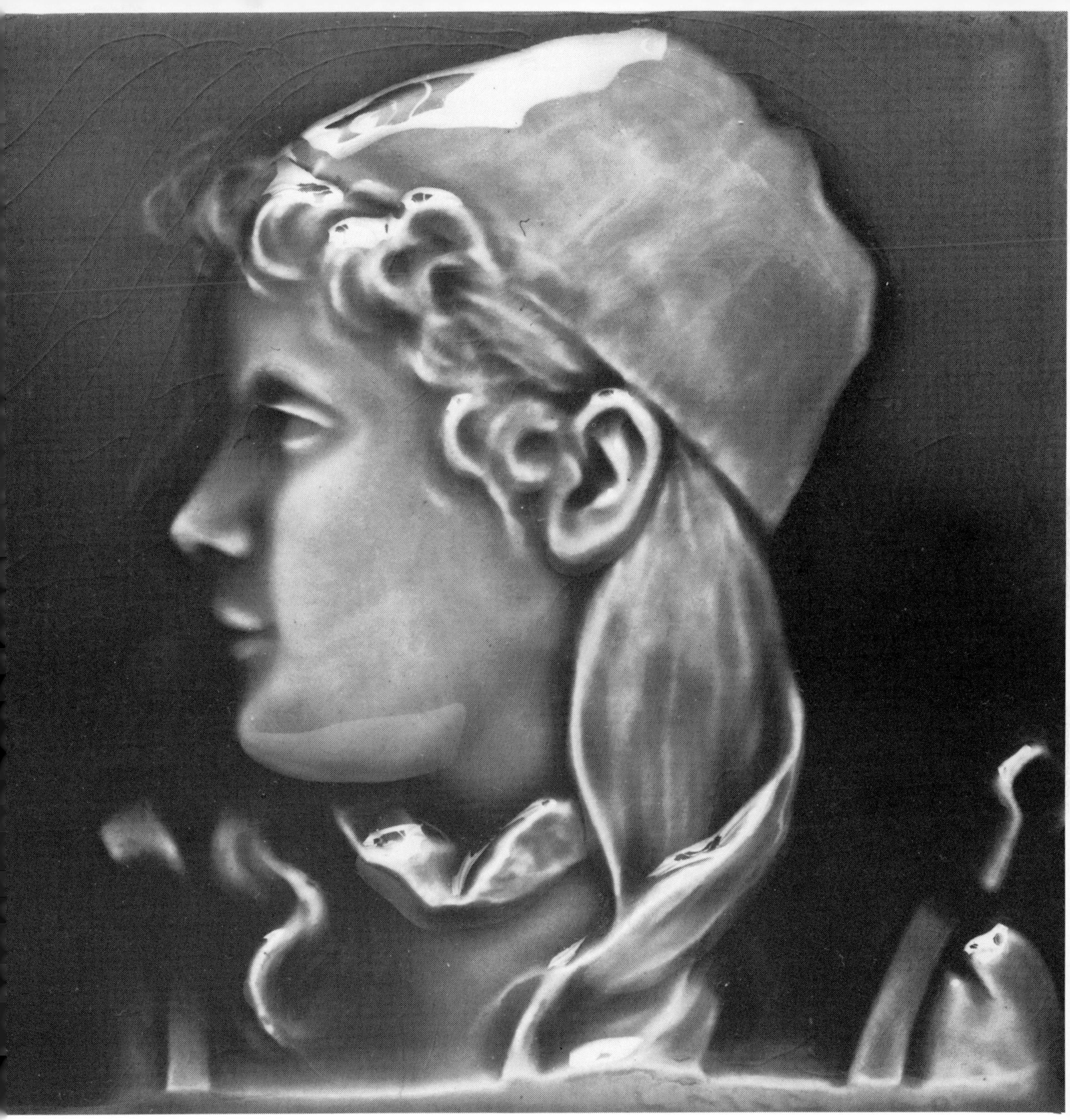

Tile with the head of a girl executed in relief, dark green translucent glaze, designed by Mary Louise McLaughlin, Kensington Tile Co., c. 1886. Cincinnati Art Museum, Ohio (*Gift of T. A. Langstroth*).

of the additional fact that the foundation of this factory was due to the intelligent and well directed efforts of a woman, the history of Rookwood, from its inception, cannot fail to have a peculiar interest for American collectors and patrons of art.'

The Rookwood Pottery was established by Mrs. Maria Longworth Nicols in 1880. The firm operated at a loss during its first nine years because of constant experimentation, remaining in business with the aid of funds provided by Mrs. Longworth Nicols' father, until it became financially independent in 1889. By 1881 the pottery was making breakfast and dinner services, pitchers, vases, wine coolers, ice tubs, umbrella stands, jars, water buckets—and tiles.

The artists employed by the Rookwood Pottery had in the main been educated at the local art schools in Cincinnati but an exception was Kataro Shirayamadani, a Japanese artist who executed some fine tiles and plaques with oriental motifs. E. P. Cranach made some interesting tiles based on *The Ballad of Isaac Abbot* and *The Ballad of Giles Scroggin's Ghost*. The Rookwood Pottery showed that it was possible to command the esteem of the American public with a product in which artistic merit was made to over-ride commercial considerations.

Another woman who featured prominently in the Cincinnati pottery world was Miss Louise McLaughlin. She became an expert pottery decorator, including in her work the designing of tiles, and it was she who encouraged other women to take an interest in decorating ceramics. In 1879 she founded the Pottery Club, a group of women who decorated pottery in their spare time. The Pottery Club was disbanded in 1890, after which a few members of the original group formed a club called the Associated Artists of Cincinnati with Miss McLaughlin as president.

Other American tile manufacturers of importance were the United States Encaustic Tile Company, Indianapolis, established in 1877; the Beaver Falls Art Tile Company, Beaver Falls, Pennsylvania, established in 1886; the Cambridge Art Tile Works, Covington, Kentucky, established in 1887; and the Robertson Art Tile Company, Morrisville, Pennsylvania, established in 1890.

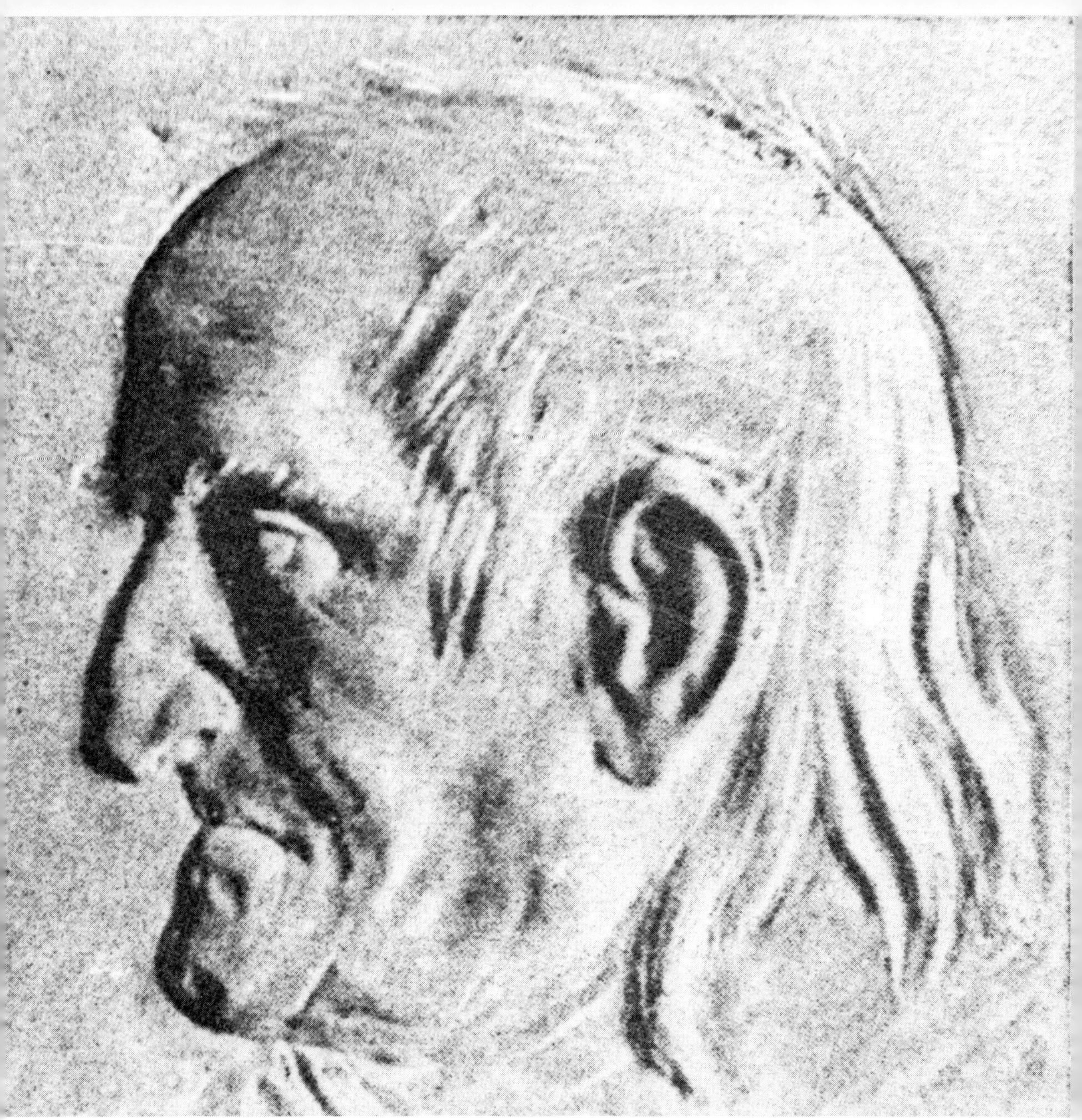

Relief tile entitled 'Old Age', The American Encaustic Tiling Co., c. 1880. *Courtesy: Leeds Central Library.*

THE STUDY OF TILES

You can add to your knowledge of the subject in three ways—by reading books about their history and manufacture, by studying tiles *in situ* and by visiting museums with good collections. Tiles in one's own collection will have been removed from their original setting but because they were, after all, a building material, it is useful to look at tiles that are still in place.

Medieval tiles can still be seen *in situ* in many medieval cathedrals and churches, but there are also comprehensive collections in the British Museum and in the Victoria and Albert Museum, both in London. Written material about them is scattered among a few books and many magazine articles, but one of the best introductions to the subject has been written by Elizabeth S. Eames and is called *Medieval Tiles—A Handbook*, published by the British Museum. It contains a brief history together with descriptions of the various production methods and decoration techniques, and the book is well illustrated.

Dutch and English Delftware tiles are not so easily found *in situ* in Britain, but the Victoria and Albert Museum has a good collection of them and provides plenty of material for study. An excellent introduction is available in Dingeman Korf's *Dutch Tiles,* while Anthony Ray's *English Delftware Tiles* is the most authorative book on that subject and also includes detailed information on the Sadler and Green transfer-printed tiles. The many illustrations in both books can be a great help to the collector.

A less specialised book that puts the history of the ceramic tile into perspective from Egyptian times up to the eighteenth century is Anne Berendsen's *Tiles—A General History*. It makes one aware that the history of tiles is a vast subject, and that the development of the English tile is only one link in a long chain. It is perhaps a pity that

A few tiles above the door can brighten up the whole facade of the house as in this instance where all the small terrace houses in Clarkson View, Woodhouse, Leeds have these attractive tiles above the doors and the windows.

the book omits proper coverage of the tile boom that took place after the eighteenth century.

Most Victorian towns in Britain provide plentiful examples of nineteenth century tiles *in situ*. Churches, public buildings, houses, shops, pubs and memorials may have either floor or wall tiles, and sometimes both. Apart from the fact that the second half of the nineteenth century saw the rise of mass production, the tile boom

Porches like these can be seen throughout Britain and house owners should count themselves lucky if they can boast of a tiled porch similar to this one in Burley Road, Leeds. The two panels with wild roses and crysanthemums are exceptionally fine.

An elaborate wall panel made of glazed inlaid tiles in St. Clement's Church, Leeds (now demolished). The tiles were made by Maw & Co. and the inscription at the top of the panel provides a useful clue to the date, c. 1871.

was also encouraged by the passing of various health acts that ensured the construction of more hygienic buildings. Strong and easy to clean, tiling was used extensively on floors and walls in town halls, public libraries, museums, hospitals, schools, railway stations and swimming pools. And as we have already noted, food shops were

Queen Victoria's arch in Beckett Park, Leeds with tiles made by Minton.

often tiled throughout for easy cleaning.

In houses, both large and small tiles were used in the hall or lobby, fireplace surround, bathroom, kitchen, and in wash stands. Their artistic qualities also led to their use for purely decorative purposes on the exteriors of buildings, for example around doorways and windows, or sometimes in the form of a string-course around the whole building. Those with letters were often used to make street names or to form inscriptions on monuments. Once one has developed an eye for spotting tiles it is amazing how many can be seen.

The most comprehensive collection of Victorian tiles is in the Gladstone Pottery Museum, Longton, Stoke-on-Trent. The tile gallery there shows the development of pottery tiles from ancient times to the present, but the majority of the exhibits concentrate on the development and expansion of the British nineteenth-century industry. The museum also shows Victorian tiles in their context in the form of fireplaces, furniture and re-assembled wall sections.

This museum incidentally admirably conveys the atmosphere of the Victorian pottery, particularly the courtyard with its bottle ovens and outbuildings, which are still being used for limited pottery production. Altogether it is a good example of a working museum in the heart of the Potteries country.

The Minton Museum in Stoke-on-Trent has only a small collection of tiles, but does have extensive documentary material in the form of original designs, pattern books and catalogues.

Another museum of interest to tile collectors is the Ironbridge Gorge Museum, Telford, that, as we have seen, rescued the plaster moulds and much of the stock of early tiles from the Maw tile

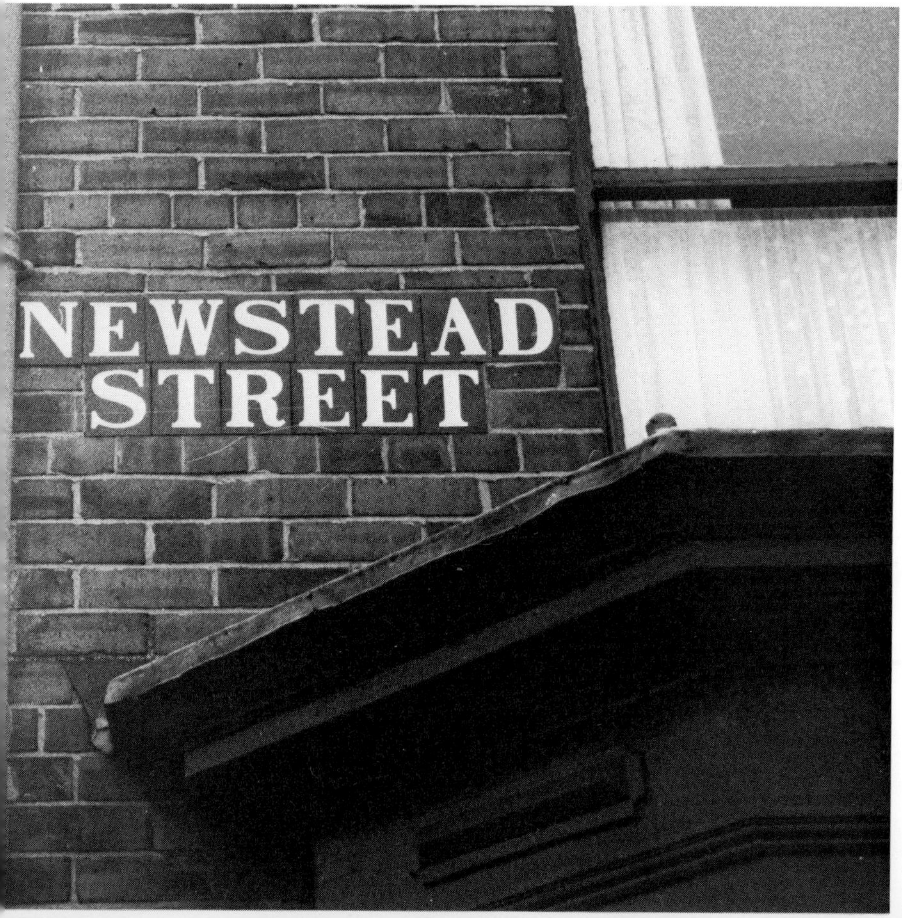

Street names made of tiles are virtually indestructable and if they get dirty a shower of rain will clean them up and they are much clearer than their cast-iron counterparts.

factory at Jackfield when it closed down. The plaster moulds and authentic tile presses have enabled the museum to make tiles using nineteenth century equipment and techniques.

Readily available written material on Victorian and Edwardian tiles is still limited to only a few books. The two that deal fully with

Plain and inlaid floor tiles can be combined to make pleasing arrangements. *Courtesy: The Mill Owner's House, Bradford Industrial Museum.*

Tiles are frequently found at the back of wash stands. This splendid example has tiles made by Minton, designed by Moyr Smith with scenes from the Waverley novels. *Courtesy: Bradford Industrial Museum.*

Late Victorian fireplaces often have tiles on either side of the fire-grate. *Courtesy: Dundee City Museum.*

A cast-iron stove decorated with Minton tiles with scenes from the Waverley novels and designed by Moyr Smith. *Courtesy: Bradford Industrial Museum.*

A coat-rack with English Art Nouveau tiles. *Tile Museum 'It Noflik Sté', Otterlo, Holland.*

this subject are W. J. Furnival's *Leadless Decorative Tiles, Faience and Mosaic* published in 1904, and J. Barnard's *Victorian Ceramic Tiles*, 1972.

Furnival's book is the Bible of anyone undertaking research into the history of nineteenth-century tiles. It received acclaim as soon as it was published, and *Connoisseur* magazine, which reviewed the book in 1904, said: 'The publication of Mr. W. J. Furnival's new book on *Leadless Decorative Tiles, Faience and Mosaic*, must certainly be regarded as a red-letter day in the annals of ceramic literature, since for the first time, this important subject covering vast periods of time, extended from 5000 B.C. to the Chicago Exhibition, spreading over many countries from China to Persia, Constantinople, Egypt to Italy, Spain, France, England and finally crossing the Atlantic for consideration of the enormous modern developments of the art in America. This extensive subject is here focused, condensed, and brought within the limits of a readable book.'

The original purpose of the book was of a philanthropic nature, because it was written to combat the lead poisoning from which so many pottery workers suffered, due to the extensive use of lead glazes throughout the industry. This is the reason why a great part of the book is taken up with recipes for leadless glazes; but it is also a technical manual on the production and decoration of tiles and as such it contains a mine of information about the nineteenth century tile industry in Britain.

Julian Barnard's *Victorian Ceramic Tiles* is the only recent publication completely devoted to the subject of Victorian tiles. It is well illustrated and soundly written, with its comprehensive list of tile manufacturer's marks making it an excellent reference book.

The collector can learn a great deal by handling tiles as well as by

The courtyard and bottle kilns of the Gladstone Pottery Museum, *Longton, Stoke-on-Trent.*

The 'Bible' for any serious student of tiles.

reading about them. Their relative weight, thickness and surface texture are all elements that play a part in assessing how, and perhaps when and where, they were made.

On-glaze decoration, for example, can sometimes be revealed only by running a finger lightly over the surface of the tile—it cannot be seen by looking at a photograph, or even at the tile itself in a glass case. Tiles are objects that can be studied from many aspects, but the tile collector will gain the most pleasure by combining an increasing visual and tactile awareness with an intellectual knowledge of the subject.

Comparing and contrasting tiles of different periods is an instructive exercise. *Top left:* Inlaid tile with knight on horseback, Dunstable Priory, 13th century. *Collection: G. K. Beaulah. Top right:* Dutch hand painted tile, manganese, 17th century. *Collection: G. K. Beaulah. Bottom left:* hand painted tile with a knight on horseback from the William Morris workshop, grey-green, c. 1875. *Collection: G. K. Beaulah. Bottom right:* lithographically printed tile with a knight on horseback design by Moyr Smith (Tennyson tiles), sepia and blue, Minton, c. 1885. *Collection: Author.*

RESTORING AND DISPLAYING

Sometimes you may get a tile in very bad condition with dirt or soot on the glaze, paint on the surface or cement still sticking to the back. This applies especially to tiles that have come directly from demolition sites. But if one knows how to go about it these tiles can be restored to something like their original state. Once you have become good at restoration it will pay you to look out for tiles among junk which a dealer has not bothered to clean as they are often considerably cheaper than the cleaned tiles.

Dirt and soot that has become ingrained in tiny scratches in the glaze can be removed with household bleaching powder. The powder is best sprinkled over a slightly wet tile and then rubbed in with the fingertips—wear rubber gloves. Rubbing the bleach along the scratches will usually remove the black lines from the surface of the tile.

If the back is dirty the same procedure can be followed, and with very stubborn dirt a piece of steel wool may be useful. Avoid using steel wool, however, on the glazed front of the tile, because it can leave tiny scratches. Very stubborn dirt on the front of the tile can be removed with paint stripper—and it goes without saying that this is the most suitable agent for removing paint.

Some tiles have many layers of paint, especially if they were the victims of the 'white-wash' wave in the 1930s, and in such cases several applications of paint stripper will be necessary, but there is always the excitement of discovering what may be underneath. Wear rubber gloves when handling paint stripper because it is a caustic material which burns the skin. When a tile is clean it should be allowed to dry normally and afterwards it can be given a rub down with a dry cloth to bring back the sheen.

Portland cement can be a real problem; if it is hard and dry it will have adhered very firmly to the back and not much can be done

Left: A tile covered with several layers of paint.

Right: The tile with all the paint removed.

about it. The only thing that might work at times is to put the tile in a potter's kiln, and heat to 700 or 800 degrees Celcius, when the different expansion rates can bring the cement off the back. However, reheating the tile may affect the decoration and glaze on the front. Low-firing enamels, for example, will burn off at that temperature. Before embarking on such a drastic step it is best to seek advice from a professional potter who knows about the nature of ceramic colours and glazes and the temperatures that affect them.

Loose and crumbling mortar can be knocked off, while grey or white plaster can be scraped away with a knife. Soaking in water can be of help in the case of old, crumbling cement, but is not much good with dry and firm cement. At all times be careful not to use too much force when removing cement, mortar or plaster from the back, in case the tile snaps.

Some tiles become covered with white crystals; these are salts and can be removed by placing the tile in a flat dish and pouring in small quantities of distilled water until the water is level with the surface of the tile. This must be done gradually, allowing each addition of water to be absorbed before more is added, as too much water poured on too suddenly will force the air out of the tile and may cause chips of glaze to come away from the surface, especially if the tile is badly crazed. Change the water a few times until all the salt has been removed and let the tile dry out naturally for several days.

Restoring broken tiles is not difficult as long as the correct procedures are followed and the right materials used. First clean the broken tile if it is dirty, taking care not to cause further damage to the edges where the tile has broken. The break may be clean, with no glaze chipped off, or it may be ragged with bits of tile and glaze missing.

After the careful cleaning and, if necessary, drying of the broken bits, the pieces should be assembled in the position in which they are going to be glued together. If the tile is in several pieces you must decide before applying any glue which pieces you are going to stick first, otherwise when you get to the last piece you may find that it is 'locked out' and cannot be inserted without your having to pull apart what you have already glued.

Use a clear, fast-drying synthetic glue and make sure when glueing two pieces that the two surfaces are exactly level with each other, for this cannot be corrected once the glue has hardened. Any excess glue which appears on the surface of the tile after two sections

An attractive display of a small collection.
Collection: J. Rumsby.

A professional display of an extensive and comprehensive collection. *Collection: G. K. Beaulah.*

have been pressed together should be removed quickly by rubbing it off with the finger. Stand the tile upright to help the adhesion of the broken parts.

If the edges are ragged or a piece of tile is missing, one can disguise this reasonably well with fillers after the glue has hardened. There are many white, non-shrinking plaster-like fillers on the market that are suitable. Use a flat bladed paint scraper to apply the filler, carefully smoothing and levelling it; then leave it to dry. If the filler shrinks, a new thin layer can be added; if it is slightly higher than the surface of the tile, rub it down with some fine sandpaper but avoid touching the glazed surface.

Using fillers on relief tiles can be slightly more complicated since the filler must follow the undulations of the surface. This can be done by putting filler along the cracks and letting it dry without smoothing it down first. Then the filler can be carefully scraped away taking care to follow all the contours, a process more like modelling than smoothing.

Once dry the filler can be tinted with colour to match the rest of the tile if this is felt desirable. Enamel paints come in a great variety of colours and if they are mixed carefully to blend in with the existing shades the tile can be restored quite acceptably. Of course it is never possible to re-create the smooth glossy surface of the glaze, but the tile will at least look whole again.

Mending a tile that has a corner missing is more difficult, but it can be done. Put the tile face down on a newspaper and lay two pieces of wood battening against the edges of the tile to form a right-angled mould for the broken corner. Line the 'mould' with thin paper to prevent the filler sticking, and then pour the filler into the mould, smoothing it down against the corner. When the filler has set and the wood is removed the paper will come off easily if it is dampened slightly.

A tile can be displayed on a little stand which is particularly suitable for the display of a favourite tile. Dutch Delftware tile, late 18th century, blue, spider's head corner ornaments. *Collection: Author.*

With a printed tile the design can be drawn on to the white filler with pencil and then painted in with enamel colours. If you find enamel paint difficult to work with you can use water colour, although this is not as permanent as enamel and dries with a matt surface. However, it can be made to look glossy if you apply a coat of clear polyurethane varnish, which has a texture very much like that of real glaze.

One of the most exciting aspects of collecting is making up a display of the tiles. The method you use will depend on the size of the collection and the amount of room available: tiles can be shown without any special mountings or fixings simply by arranging them along a shelf or ledge.

A slightly more ambitious method is to fix several display ledges on to a large piece of black, grey or white-painted chipboard, positioning them slightly wider apart than the height of the largest tiles.

Arrange the tiles according to themes, decorative techniques or stylistic influences and design. Tiles can also be hung on the wall, using special wire attachments—group them in sets of four to bring out the design aspects of the pattern.

Another effective method of showing off a set of four tiles is by mounting them in a frame. If a wooden frame is used make sure that the edges are flush with the tiles, as an overlapping edge would obscure part of the tiles. You can also make a frame of plaster or polyurethane foam. A plaster backing is easy to make, cheap and strong, provided that the panel is kept in a dry atmosphere. To make it, face the tiles down on a flat surface and fit four lengths of wood battening, $1\frac{1}{2}$ inches (4 cm) deeper than the tiles are, around the tiles to make a rough mould. Dampen the tiles and place a piece of wire mesh, slightly smaller than their total area, over them to reinforce the plaster. Pour in the plaster to a depth of 1 inch ($2\frac{1}{2}$ cm). A U-shaped metal hook placed in position before the plaster begins to harden will set firm in the plaster and you will be able to use it to hang the display on the wall. Allow the plaster to harden before removing the battening mould.

A polyurethane foam mix is available which, when mixed (it consists of two components), forms a rigid frame strong enough to support four tiles. The procedure for making the frame is similar to that for plaster, except that one does not dampen the tiles, and it is advisable to cover the wooden frame around the tiles with polythene to prevent the foam sticking to it.

The foam expands after it has been mixed and poured on to the tiles, so to keep the foam surface level, a piece of glass lined with polythene should be placed on top. It will be appreciated that this type of backing needs careful thought and preparation as it is technically more complex than plaster, but it is much stronger and lighter and will not be affected by damp.

Store tiles that cannot be displayed in an upright position, one behind the other, in a stout cardboard box with a strong base. To prevent any damage, interleave the tiles with paper.

Cataloguing is another important aspect of collecting. Buy some adhesive labels and a notebook, then give each tile an identifying number; write it first on a label for the back of the tile, then enter it in the notebook with the particulars of the tile, including such information as decoration technique, colour, subject-matter, design

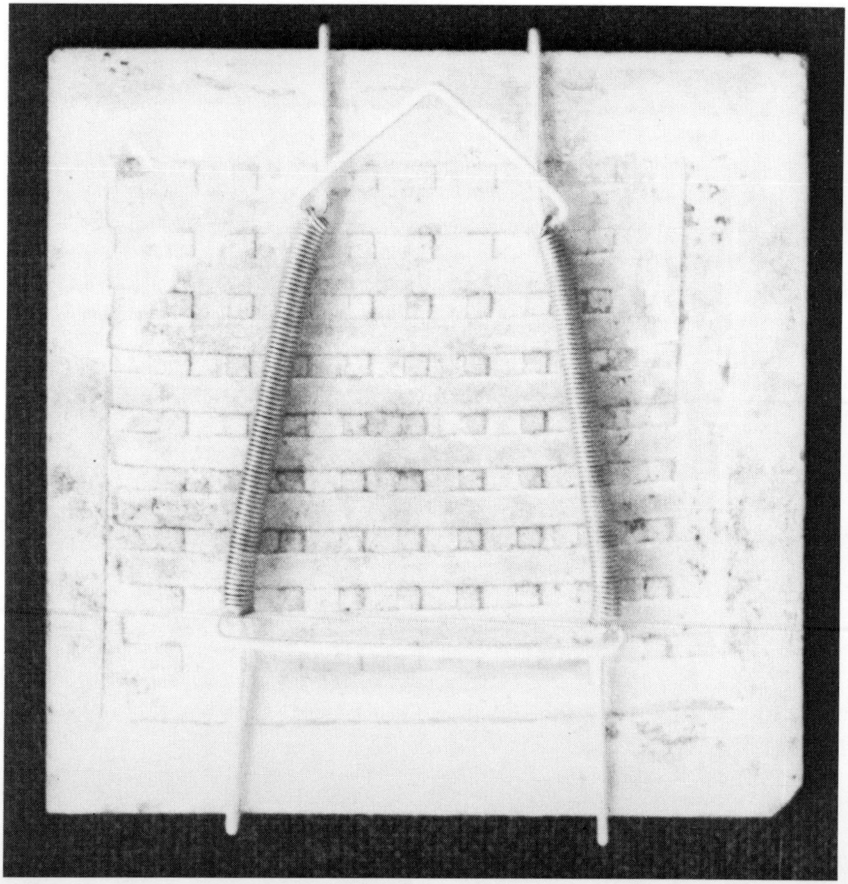

A wire attachment on the back of a tile makes it possible to hang it on the wall.

A wrought iron lamp-stand specially made to display three polychrome 17th century Dutch tiles. *Collection: Mr. & Mrs. T. van Lemen.*

The back of a dust pressed inlaid tile with the Wedgwood trade mark stamped in the centre, c. 1885. *Collection: Author.*

more clue-hunting is necessary.

A registration number may appear in the form of a diamond-shaped mark containing letters and numbers; this type was used between 1842 and 1883. After 1883 the number appears as a series of consecutive numbers prefixed with the letters 'Rd.' (the abbreviation for 'registered').

Registration marks and numbers were issued by the Patent Office in London to give the tile maker some protection for a limited period from having the design of a tile copied, and the marks can be traced back to give the maker's name and the date of the tile. In order to do this one has to go to the Public Records Office at Kew in London, which is purpose built for the quick finding of information with the aid of computers.

A diamond registration mark can easily be decoded with the right key and will give you the day, month and year of registration. Tiles

The back of a dust pressed wall tile made by Wedgwood. The raised bars would assist fixing the tile to the wall, c. 1890. *Collection: G. K. Beaulah.*

fall into the index category BT (short for Board of Trade). With the right index and the date of the tile it is now possible to use the computers to pick out two books that you need, one containing the date of the registration plus the names of the manufacturers, and the other illustrating registered items such as iron-work, wallpaper and textiles as well as tiles. The book in which you can discover the name of the maker also gives a number with which you can track down the design of the tile in the illustrated book. These are usually in the form of black and white drawings, but they provide a useful check that the name of the manufacturer you found is indeed the one who made your tile.

A printed number that does not look like a registration is probably a catalogue number. Certain major libraries and museums, particularly in the Potteries area, have tile catalogues that can be seen on request, and by browsing through these one can identify a

Above left: The back of a hand-made inlaid tile by Minton. The diamond registration mark with the letter A in the right hand corner gives us the date 1871. *Collection: Author.*
Above right: The round holes in the backs of inlaid tiles made from plastic clay help to dry the tile more quickly and also help to fix the tile to the floor or the wall. *Collection: Author.*
Below: The instrument which the tile maker used to press a series of holes in the back of an inlaid tile made from plastic clay. *Gladstone Pottery Museum.*

tile and therefore the maker. If one is lucky enough to find a tile in a catalogue which resembles a tile in one's collection, the printed number on the back should correspond with the number given to the tile.

Certain tiles have numbers and letters painted in glaze on the back, which were probably simply stock or batch numbers.

Some manufacturers, such as Minton, did occasionally put their own year marks on the back of inlaid tiles, thus giving them a precise date. Year marks are little symbols, and the key to the Minton marks can be found in most dictionaries of pottery and porcelain. But it must be understood that the use of these year marks on tiles is rare.

Dating tiles can be a hazardous business, but there are various ways of getting an approximate idea. Those with registration numbers and marks give a fairly accurate date, although it must be borne in mind that the tile could have been in production for several years at least after registration. Unmarked tiles can be dated with the aid of a catalogue, because the date of the catalogue itself will give an approximate fix for any tile found in it.

If you obtain any tiles from demolition sites the date of the building will provide a pointer to the date of the tile. An experienced collector might even find certain stylistic features a help. For instance, most Art Nouveau tiles were made at the beginning of this century, while tiles inspired by the Arts and Crafts movement can be dated between 1880 and 1900—but one must always be ready for surprises.

Left: The back of a hand-made Copeland tile. It can be clearly seen that a comb has been pulled through the clay in two directions. *Collection: G. K. Beaulah.*

Right: The back of dust pressed tile with the trade mark of Sherwin & Cotton in the centre. *Collection: Author.*

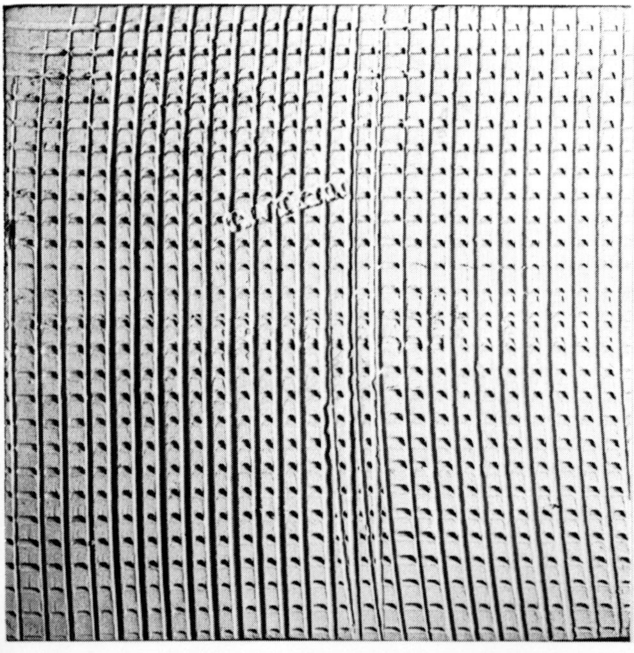

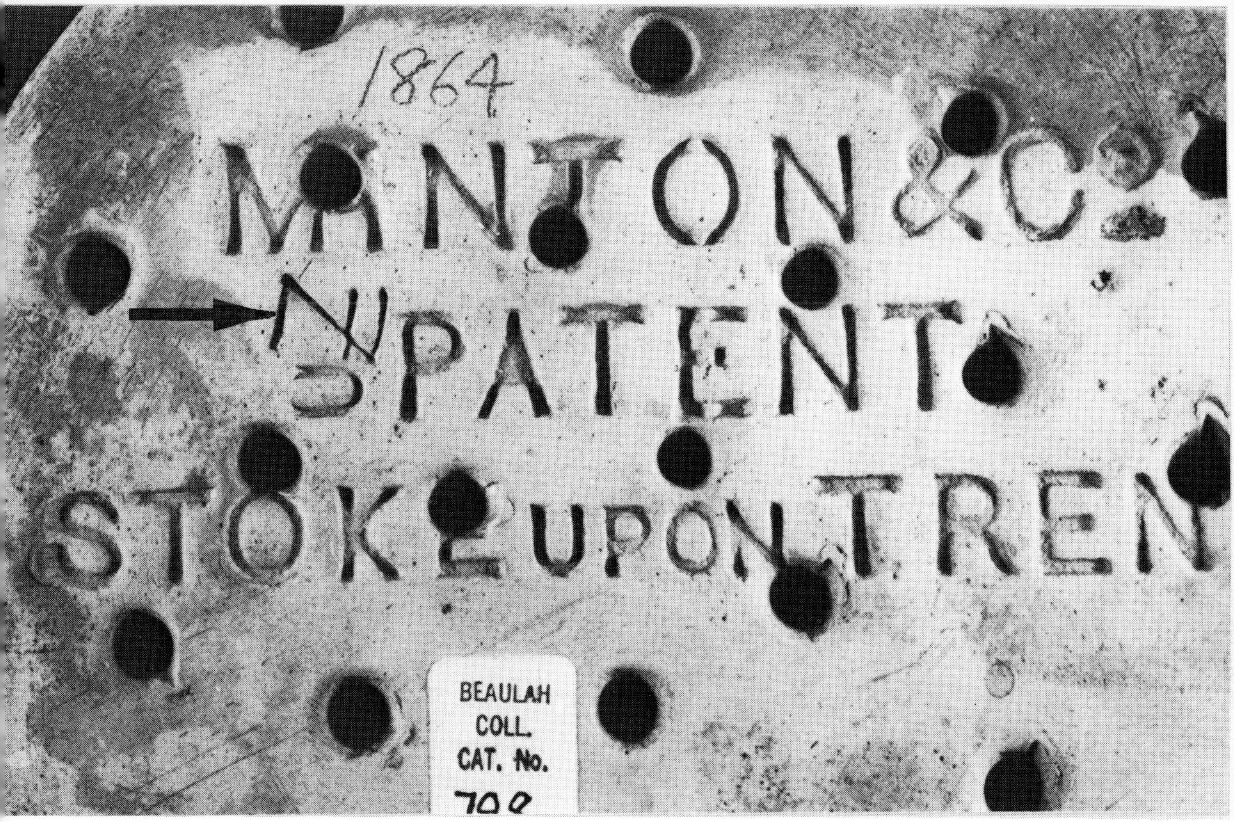

Above: The back of this inlaid tile made from plastic clay has a Minton year mark (see black arrow) impressed in it. This particular year mark stands for 1864. *Collection: G. K. Beaulah.*

Below: Registration marks can appear in different shapes and forms. *Left:* diamond registration mark as used between 1868 and 1883. *Middle:* Although since 1884 registration marks appear as consecutive numbers, the first numbers still appear in a diamond shaped figure. *Right:* A registration number like this is found on many tiles after 1884.

This panel posed an interesting problem as far as the date and the maker were concerned. At a first glance the panel looks late Victorian judging by the dress of the girl, but an investigation led to the following information. The panel came from a dairy shop in Dundee, which was owned by the Buttercup Dairy Co. This firm had their head office in Leith, Edinburgh and owned many dairy shops throughout Scotland. All their shops had a panel of tiles showing a girl feeding buttercups to a cow and the source for this picture was a Victorian painting which hung in the head office in Leith. The tile blanks were made by T. & R. Boote Ltd.,Waterloo Pottery, Burslem and the tiles were decorated by J. Duncan, a tile decorator with premises in Glasgow. The figures are tube-lined and coloured in by hand in shades of green, pink, blue, yellow and white. The panel was made in 1924. *Collection: Author.*

Far right: Tile catalogues can be very useful in identifying and dating the makers of unmarked tiles. This page is from a Minton catalogue of c. 1885, showing a fine range of 6 and 8 inch tiles. *Courtesy: Minton Museum, Royal Doulton Tableware Ltd.*

MINTONS (Limited):—CHINA WORKS: STOKE-UPON-TRENT, and 28, WALBROOK, LONDON

Tiles Richly Glazed and Decorated with Enamels

FOR FLOWER BOXES, FRIEZES, WALLS AND OTHER ARCHITECTURAL DECORATION, FURNITURE, FIRE PLACES, &c.

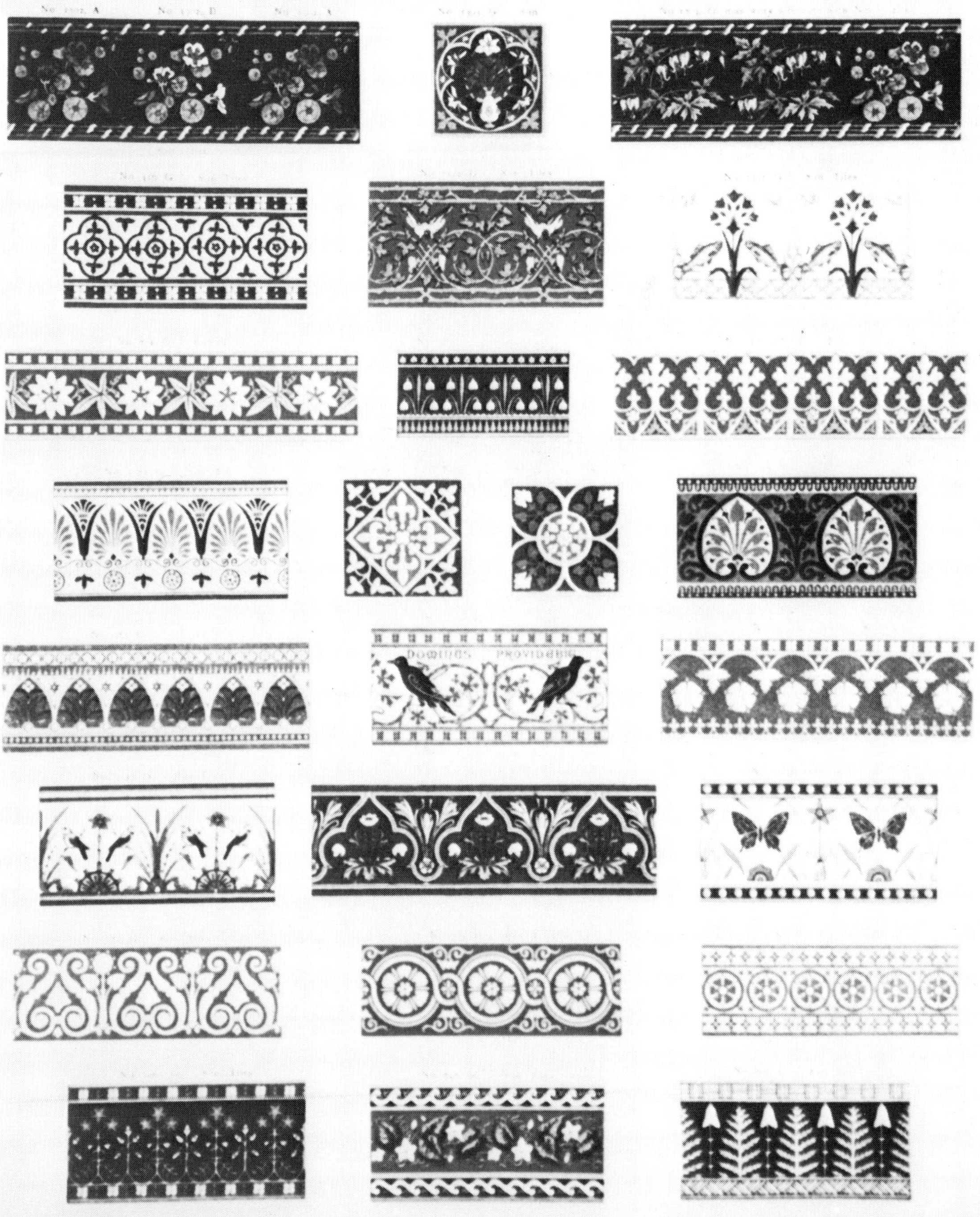

Scale ... to a foot
Inches

POSTAL ADDRESS
MINTONS (Limited):—
CHINA WORKS,
STOKE-UPON-TRENT.

Atkinson Brothers, Lithographers, Hanley

Diamond Registration Marks

Year Code 1842–67			*Year Code 1868–83*		*Month Code 1842–83*	
1842 X	1855 E	*1842–67*	1868 X	1881 E	January	C
1843 H	1856 L	a class	1869 H	1882 L	February	G
1844 C	1857 K	b year	1870 C	1883 K	March	W
1845 A	1858 B	c month	1871 A		April	H
1846 I	1859 M	d day	1872 I		May	E
1847 F	1860 Z	e bundle	1873 F		June	M
1848 U	1861 R		1874 U		July	I
1849 S	1862 O	*1868–83*	1875 S		August	R
1850 V	1863 G	a class	1876 V		September	D
1851 P	1864 N	b day	1877 P		October	B
1852 D	1865 W	c bundle	1878 D		November	K
1853 Y	1866 Q	d year	1879 Y		December	A
1854 J	1867 T	e month	1880 J			

Registration Numbers 1884–1909

1884–1	1897–291241
1885–19754	1898–311658
1886–40480	1899–331707
1887–64520	1900–351202
1888–90483	1901–368154
1889–116648	1902–385500
1890–141273	1903–402500
1891–163767	1904–420000
1892–185713	1905–447000
1893–205240	1906–471000
1894–224720	1907–494000
1895–246975	1908–519000
1896–268392	1909–550000

GLOSSARY

AEROGRAPHY: A method by which tiles are decorated with the aid of an air-brush, and colours are sprayed through a stencil on to the tile.
ARTS AND CRAFTS MOVEMENT: A movement of British designers and architects who during the second half of the 19th century changed the nature of Victorian design by making it more true to the surface for which it was designed. Work done by hand, flat design and simplification of natural form are the hallmarks of this movement.
ART NOUVEAU: A new form of decorative art at the end of the 19th century, easily recognised by its use of sinuous and sensuous lines.
ART TILE: A name used during the second half of the 19th century for tiles showing the influence of contemporary design movements, like the Arts and Crafts movement and Art Nouveau, and which often have a special aesthetic quality.
BIANCO-SOPRA-BIANCO: White-on-white.
BISCUIT: A tile that has been fired once.
BODY: Main substance of a tile.
CERAMIC COLOUR: A colour that will withstand the fierce heat of the kiln.
CHINOISERIE: A name given to 18th and 19th-century objects and designs that show influences from the Far East.
CLASSICISM: A term used throughout the visual arts to denote the influence of Greek and Roman art.
DELFTWARE TILE: Tile dipped in tin glaze at biscuit stage on which a decoration is painted by hand. This decoration is called 'in-glaze' because it sinks into the tin glaze during the second firing.
DUST CLAY: Finely powdered clay with a low moisture content.
DUST PRESSING: The compressing with great force of powdered clay in a press.

ENAMEL: A ceramic colour which can be painted on a glazed surface and be permanently fixed to it by means of a low temperature firing.
ENCAUSTIC: Another word for 'inlaid'.
FAIENCE: Originally tin glazed ware, but during the second half of the 19th century the term was used to indicate architectural ceramics that had been moulded and glazed. The word comes from the name of the Italian town Faenza.
GLAZE: The glassy coating on pottery.
GREEN TILE: An unfired tile.
IN-GLAZE: See 'Delftware Tile.'
INTAGLIO: Relief in reverse
KILN: Oven in which pottery is fired.
LEAD GLAZE: Glossy transparent glaze made from lead and therefore highly poisonous in an unfired state.
LITHOGRAPHY: Printing from prepared stone slab. The pattern is drawn on the stone with greasy crayon which rejects water. The stone is then wetted, and an oily ink is rolled on, which is rejected by the wet stone but sticks to the design executed in greasy crayon. A sheet of paper (transfer tissue) is now pressed on which picks up the ink and can then be transferred to the surface of the tile while still tacky.
LOCK BACK: A deeply undercut indentation on the back of a tile which 'locks' the cement. Sherwin and Cotton were the first to make tiles with lock backs.
LUSTRE: A ceramic colour that through the introduction of smoke in the kiln during the firing turns into a thin film of metal. Copper and silver lustre are the most common.
MAJOLICA: Originally earthenware with white tin glaze painted with bright colours, but the term is also used for relief tiles with opaque or translucent glazes. The word comes from the name of Majorca, the island which used to be a major centre of painted pottery during the 15th century.
MANGANESE: An oxide producing mauve.
MASTER DESIGN: Original design from which copies are taken.
MOULD: A matrix in which a cast is made.
MUFFLE KILN: Special kiln for low temperature firings.
NEO-GOTHIC: The revival of medieval design in the 19th century.

ON-GLAZE: A decoration executed on the glaze with enamels.
PETIT-FEU: French term for low temperature firing.
PLASTIC CLAY: Ordinary wet clay.
POUNCE: Little cloth bag filled with black powder which is patted over a perforated drawing for getting a design on a tile. The little dots serve as a guide for hand-painting.
RELIEF: Raised design.
SGRAFFITO: Scratching through the top surface of two layers of clay and revealing the colour of the bottom layer.
STENCIL: A piece of paper, cardboard or metal with a design cut out of it through which colour can be applied.
SLIP: Thin liquid clay.
TILE BLANK: Undecorated tile.
TIN GLAZE: A glaze made by adding tin to a lead glaze, and which when fired becomes an opaque white.
TRANSLUCENT GLAZE: A transparent glaze to which colour has been added, while the surface to which it has been applied shows through.
TRANSFER PRINTING: The transfer of a printed image from a metal plate or lithographic stone to pottery by means of transfer tissue.
TUBE-LINING: The piping of delicate lines of slip on to a tile.
UNDER-GLAZE: A printed or painted decoration under a transparent glaze.

BIBLIOGRAPHY

A. Berendsen *Tiles—A General History,* Faber and Faber, 1967

E. S. Eames *Medieval Tiles—A Handbook,* British Museum, 1968

J. Wright *Mediaeval Floor Tiles,* John Baker, 1975

B. Rackham *Dutch Tiles—The Van Den Bergh Gift,* Victoria and Albert Museum, 1931

D. Korf *Dutch Tiles,* Merlin Press, 1963

C. H. de Jonge *Dutch Tiles,* Pall Mall Press, 1971

P. Clarijs *Een Huis Vol Tegels,* Contact, Amsterdam, 1970

A. Ray *English Delftware Tiles,* Faber and Faber, 1973

L. Jewitt *Ceramic Art of Great Britain,* 2 vols., 1878

L. Lefevre *Architectural Pottery,* 1900

W. J. Furnival *Leadless Decorative Tiles, Faience and Mosaic,* 1904

J. Barnard *Victorian Ceramic Tiles,* Studio Vista, 1972

A. Lane *A Guide to the Collection of Tiles,* Victoria and Albert Museum, 1939

R. Pinkham *Catalogue of Pottery by William De Morgan,* Victoria and Albert Museum, 1973

W. G. Gaunt and M. D. E. Clayton-Stamm *William De Morgan,* Studio Vista, 1971

E. A. Barber *The Pottery and Porcelain of the United States,* 1901

C. T. Davis *A Practical Treatise on the Manufacture of Brick, Tiles and Terra-Cotta,* 1895

G. A. Godden *Encyclopedia of British Pottery and Porcelain Marks,* 1964

J. Larney *Restoring Ceramics,* Barrie and Jenkins, 1975

D. Hamilton *Architectural Ceramics,* Thames and Hudson, 1978

INDEX